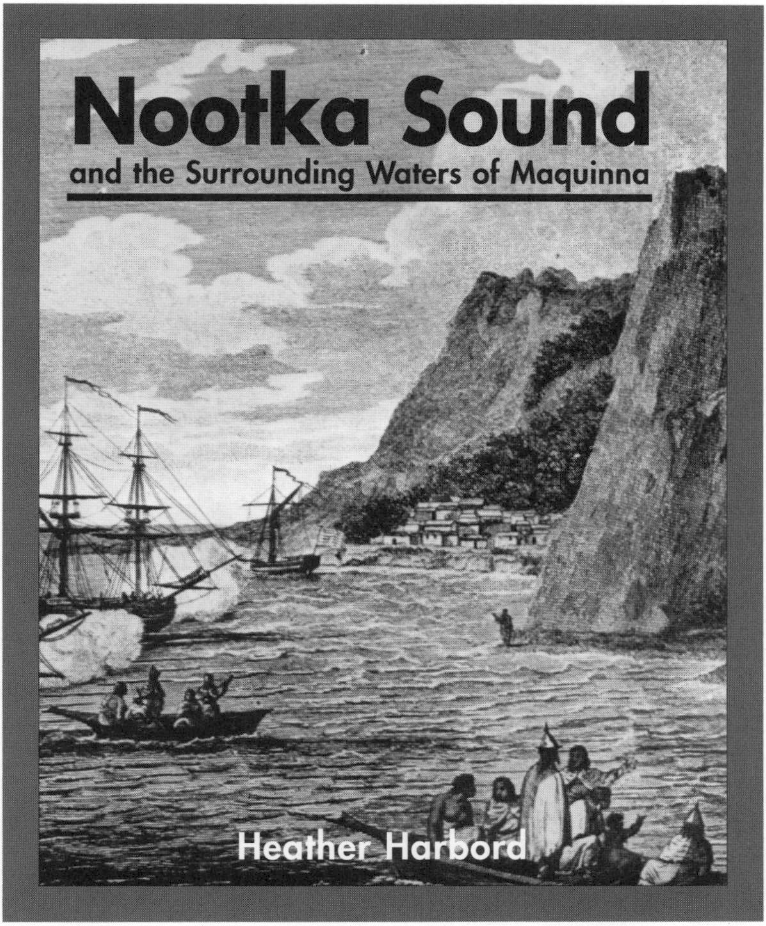

# Nootka Sound

## and the Surrounding Waters of Maquinna

Heather Harbord

HERITAGE HOUSE

**Canadian Cataloguing in Publication Data**
Harbord, Heather, 1939–
Nootka Sound and the surrounding waters of Maquinna

Includes index.
ISBN 1-895811-03-1

1. Nootka Sound (B.C.)—Description and travel. 2. Esperanza Inlet (B.C.)—Description and travel. I. Title
FC3845.N65H37 1996 917.11'2 C95-910682-0
F1089.N8H37 1996

First Edition 1996

Design and Typesetting by Cecilia Hirczy Welsford

Heritage House Publishing Company Limited
#8 – 17921 55th Avenue, Surrey B.C. V3S 6C4

Printed in Canada

## DEDICATION

*To*

*Angie O'Keefe and Carol Gramlich*

*whose annual encouragement kept me on track*


## ACKNOWLEDGMENTS

Thanks are due to many people in Gold River, Tahsis, Zeballos, Kyuquot, and other ports where the *M.V. Uchuck III* calls. Both their willingness to provide information and contribute photographs has helped me greatly. My gratitude extends to many people on Vancouver Island and near my Powell River home who provided additional facts and opinions. I enjoyed all our conversations and appreciate your assistance.

Special thanks are due to Margaret Waddington for checking the historical facts surrounding the Nootka Controversy.

Thanks to all my kayaking and canoeing partners. I will never forget the scintillating conversations at 5:00 a.m., the salmon suppers and other cooperative meals, the help with carrying my kayak up and down the beach, and the singsongs for attentive audiences of sea otters.

Thanks to my editors, Rodger Touchie, Joanne Richardson, and Art Downs, who didn't give up in despair, and to three instructors at the Sechelt Writers Festival, Isabel Nanton, Andreas Schroeder, and Daniel Wood, who encouraged me to keep trying.


* * * * *

Although every effort has been made to ensure that facts presented in this book are accurate and up-to-date, the author and publisher make no guarantee as to the accuracy of information contained herein. Likewise, the author and publisher assume no responsibility for injury or damage to one's person, vehicle, or boat resulting from travel in areas described in this book. Go prepared for wilderness conditions and use common sense. Know your personal limitations and the capabilities of your vehicle and boat. Mariners are advised to consult official sailing directions and nautical charts.

Heritage House acknowledges the support of Canadian Heritage and the Cultural Services Branch of British Columbia. Historic illustrations are from the Vancouver Public Library Collection.

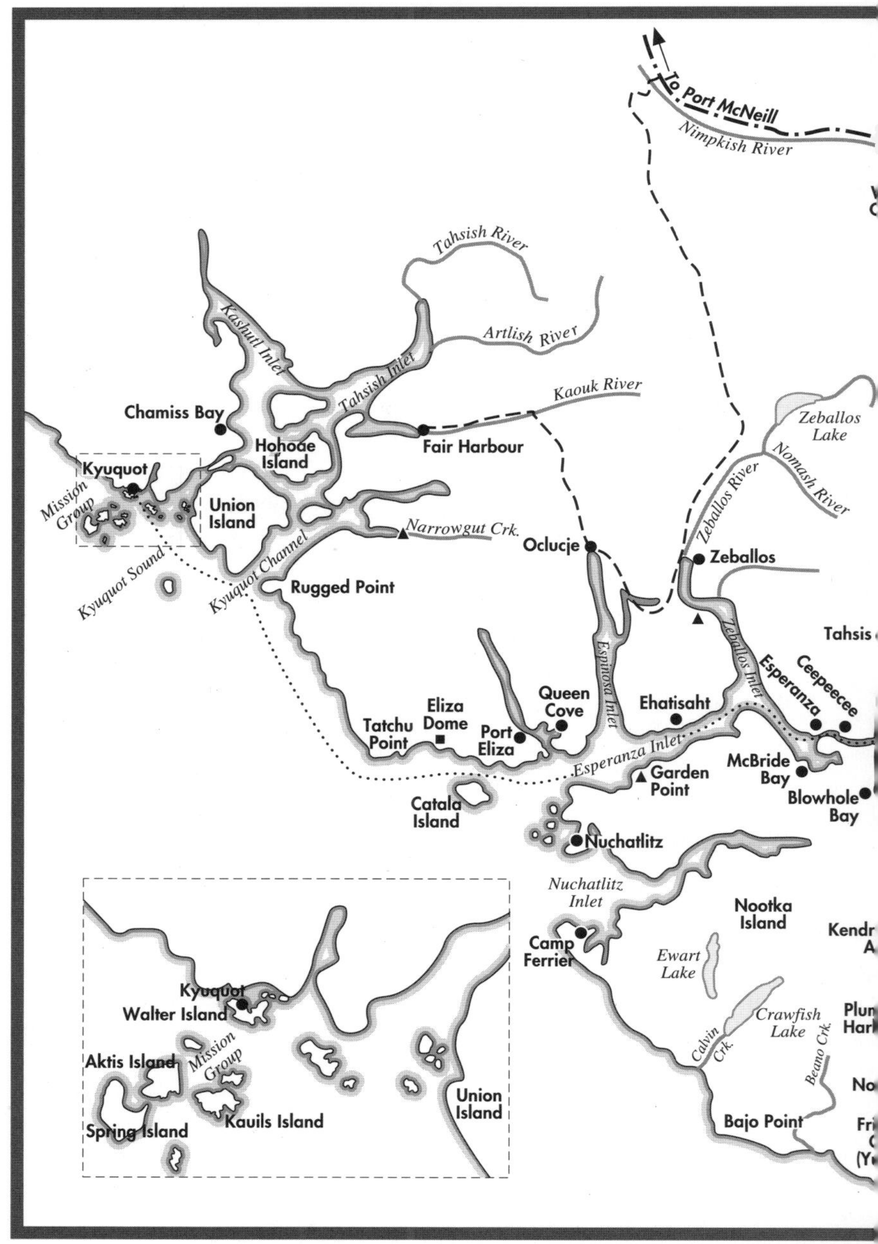
To Port McNeill
Nimpkish River
Tahsish River
Artlish River
Kashutl Inlet
Tahsish Inlet
Kaouk River
Zeballos Lake
Nomash River
Zeballos River
Chamiss Bay
Hohoae Island
Fair Harbour
Kyuquot
Mission Group
Union Island
Narrowgut Crk.
Oclucje
Zeballos
Kyuquot Sound
Kyuquot Channel
Rugged Point
Tahsis
Espinosa Inlet
Zeballos Inlet
Esperanza
Ceepeecee
Queen Cove
Ehatisaht
Tatchu Point
Eliza Dome
Port Eliza
Esperanza Inlet
McBride Bay
Garden Point
Blowhole Bay
Catala Island
Nuchatlitz
Nuchatlitz Inlet
Nootka Island
Camp Ferrier
Ewart Lake
Crawfish Lake
Calvin Crk.
Beano Crk.
Bajo Point
Walter Island
Aktis Island
Spring Island
Kauils Island

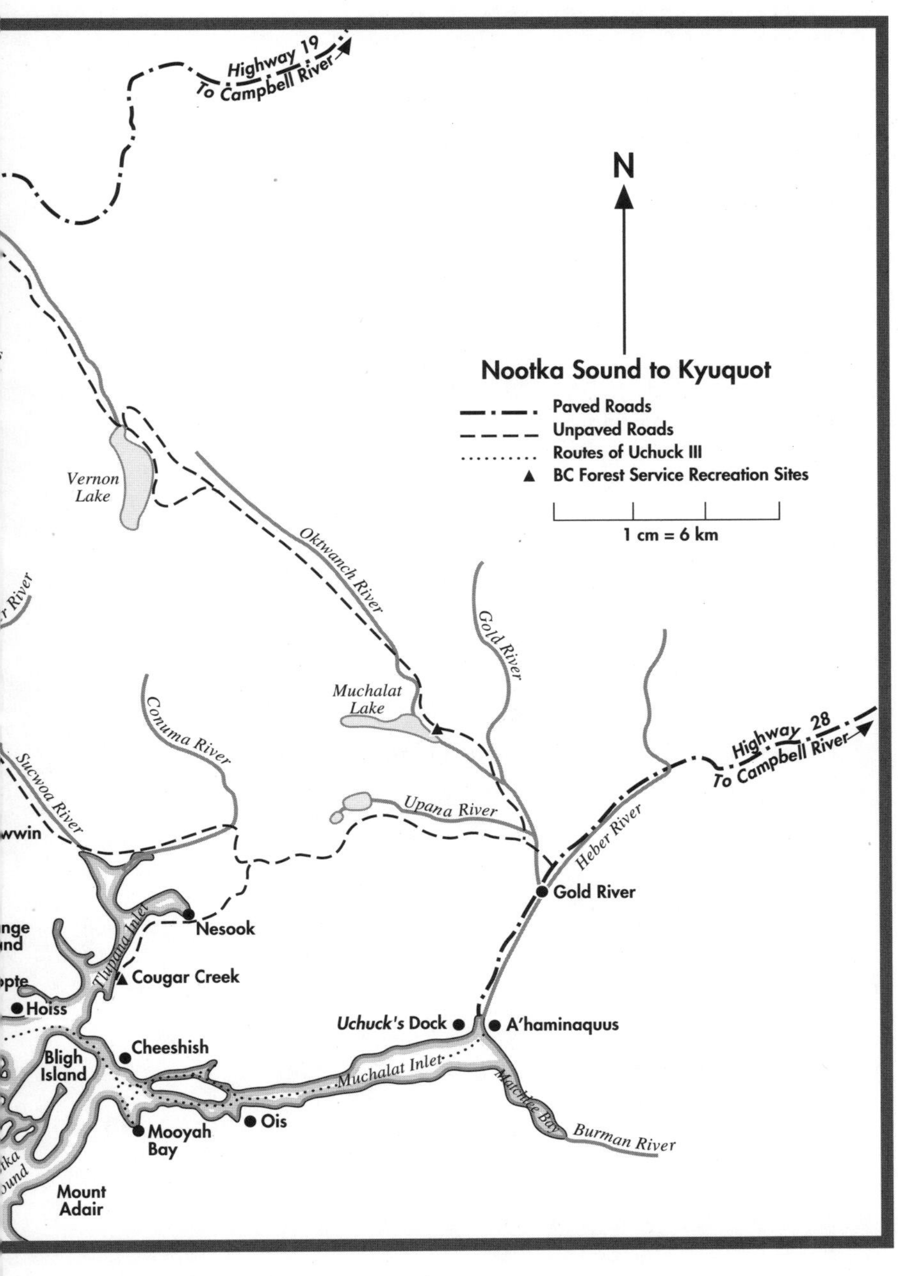
Nootka Sound to Kyuquot
Paved Roads
Unpaved Roads
Routes of Uchuck III
BC Forest Service Recreation Sites
1 cm = 6 km
N
Highway 19
To Campbell River
Highway 28
To Campbell River
Vernon Lake
Oktwanch River
Gold River
Muchalat Lake
Conuma River
Sucwoa River
Upana River
Heber River
Gold River
Nesook
Tlupana Inlet
Cougar Creek
Hoiss
Uchuck's Dock
A'haminaquus
Cheeshish
Bligh Island
Muchalat Inlet
Matchlee Bay
Burman River
Mooyah Bay
Ois
Mount Adair

# CONTENTS

# IN THE BEGINNING

"There's a boat that will take you and your sea kayak out to Friendly Cove and pick you up again further along its route," my friend told me in July 1979. I took his advice and, since that time, have been drawn back again and again to the wild beauty, the sheltered waters, and the rich historical tapestry of Nootka Sound. For modern explorers a very real part of discovering Nootka is discovering its history — this is where British Columbia began.

These waters on the West Coast of Vancouver Island were visited by Captain James Cook during his third and last voyage round the world. In 1778, he was the first European to land in the Pacific Northwest and was welcomed by Maquinna, the dominant chief of the region, with gifts of lustrous sea otter furs.

For twenty-five years following Cook's discovery, Nootka was the focal point of European interest in this remote corner of the Pacific. Maquinna's innocent gift of sea otter pelts started a stampede of bounty hunters from distant shores.

The sea otter hunt was a short-lived saga of indiscriminant slaughter which ultimately resulted in the eradication of this species from the British Columbia coast. Before it was over, the land of Maquinna was scarred forever. Finally, in 1803, responding to the latest humiliation, warriors of the great chief burned the American ship *Boston* and, after killing the other twenty-five crew members, took John Jewitt and John Thompson captive. Three years later, after his rescue, Jewitt went to Massachusetts and wrote his *Narrative*, a document describing his enslavement. This document would imbed the name Nootka in the history of the Pacific Northwest forever.

History is only one facet that lures tourists and adventurers to Nootka Sound today. As the most sheltered part of the west coast and rich in salmon, this area is fast replacing the Strait of Georgia as a sports fishing mecca. The former pilchard cannery site where I camped in 1979 is now the oldest and most exclusive sports fishing camp in the area. Guests are flown in from Campbell River and the U.S. for a week-long stay with all meals, equipment and guides provided. Since 1990, many similar establishments have opened, especially in Tlupana Inlet. In July and August salmon weighing 11–18 kilograms (25–40 pounds) are caught.

*Off on another adventure, the author is lowered over the side of the* Uchuck.

A fishing expedition is not the only way to see the area. The passenger and freight boat that serves the sound, the *M.V. Uchuck III*, carries about 1,500 passengers a year on its weekly routes. Many tourists settle for a day trip to Tahsis or Friendly Cove, where Captain Cook went ashore. The more adventurous take the overnight trip to Kyuquot (pronounced Ky-you-kit). Kayakers and canoeists, like myself, are dropped off to camp along the way. Our launches and pick-ups from pallets slung over the side of the *Uchuck* provide much entertainment for those left on board. Although Esperanza Inlet and Kyuquot Sound are not strictly "waters of Maquinna," I discuss them in the book because the *Uchuck* traverses them. Similarly, the logging roads which link these waterways are also discussed.

Every time I come to the Nootka Sound area, there are new things to savour. Once I took with me the *Narrative* of John Jewitt, mentioned above. By kayak, I went to many of the places he described and met the descendants of his captors. Another time, I drove the logging roads linking Gold River, Tahsis, and Zeballos while reading pioneer logger Gordon Gibson's autobiographical account of adventures in the early forest industry and prospector Walter Guppy's description of the Zeballos mines.

It is not only the human history which has repeatedly drawn me back; the wildlife holds endless fascination. Bird life is abundant and vocal. Bald eagles wheel and chitter in the tree tops. Ravens and crows noisily attack any food or shiny material left unattended. Song sparrows, robins, and thrushes seem to sing all day. From our kayaks, my friends and I often see grey whales close by. Recently, the sea otters, which have been extinct along the B.C. coast since the early 1800s, have been successfully reintroduced.

Although the waterways have always provided the easiest access to the area, landbound visitors can enjoy saltchuck activities from ocean-side campsites and picnic grounds like Fair Harbour, Little Espinosa, Zeballos, Tahsis and the popular Cougar Creek. The roads around the sound provide spectacular views over the inlets and access to many small trout-filled lakes. Muchalat Lake, 15 km (9 miles) from Gold River, is one of my favourite places for camping and swimming. In the early morning and evening the still water mirrors the mountains. I think of this as an ideal place for children to catch their first fish and eat it panfried while a nearby loon announces sundown.

Section 1 chronicles the rich history of Nootka Sound. Section 2 introduces a contemporary but historic ship, the *M.V. Uchuck*, which has been a critical link in the transportation and shipping needs of the territory. It is only the *Uchuck*, a web of logging roads, and two small regional airlines that provide non-boaters access to this wonderful land. Section 3 takes you on some of my favourite kayak trips. And for those who want to do their own exploring, I summarize accommodations, campsites and facilities, useful contacts, maps, charts, and metric conversions. Under Further Reading, I include an annotated bibliography.

*Three turn-of-the-century photographs by Edward Curtis show both the majesty of the Nuu-Chah-Nulth peoples who lived on Vancouver Island's west coast and the intricacy of their cedar-bark clothes. The sketch in the middle is a the work of Captain James Cook's artist, John Webber, completed during their 1778 visit to Friendly Cove. Fifteen distinct family groups of First Nations peoples have lived here for thousands of years.*

# Chapter 1

# EXPLORERS AND EXPLOITERS FROM COOK TO JEWITT

The history of British Columbia begins at Nootka. More than half a century before the Hudson's Bay Company established Fort Victoria, Nootka was the site of discovery, confrontation, economic pillage, and international accord. Many sea captains, some honourable, some borderline pirates, sailed into Nootka Sound, and even the leadership of a great warrior chief could not protect the local natives from the invasion of the outside world.

Ironically, more than most parts of British Columbia, Nootka remains much as it was 200 years ago. History has left many marks, but Nootka Sound is still defined by the land and the aboriginal peoples.

## THE FIRST NATIONS

Legends say the Mowachaht have always lived in Nootka Sound and archaeologists confirm a pattern of unbroken settlement dating back 4,300 years. Excavations have been conducted at Yuquot, (Friendly Cove,) and other sites around Nootka Sound.

In pre-European times, people spent their summers in small coastal villages throughout the inlets and along the outer coast. Each family group had its own tyee or head man. Before the winter gales, they gathered in sheltered locations such as Matchlee, Hoiss, Coopte, and Tahsis. These village groupings formed loose confederacies usually dominated by one or more tyees. Yuquot was such a confederacy, and, to this day, its dominant tyee bears the title of Maquinna.

For the Mowachaht, life at Yuquot was comfortable. Food was plentiful and trade with other villages was profitable. The people could stand on the headland with the ocean at their back, knowing the forest-covered mountains and islands were their domain. Provided they fulfilled the necessary rituals, they were confident the land would look after them as it had since time began. Then came the white man, and this centuries-old lifestyle was altered forever.

## EARLY VOYAGERS DID NOT STOP

The Russians and Spaniards were the first to send ships to the Northwest Coast of North America. The Spaniards claimed possession under a papal decree which split the Americas between Spain and Portugal. Other countries, such as England, took little notice of this decree. From Russia, Bering and Chirikov explored the Aleutian Islands and the Alaska Panhandle in 1741.

**_Drake's Voyage Not Far Enough_**

*Sir Francis Drake rounded Cape Horn and sailed up the west coast of North America to somewhere between 43° and 48° north latitude before turning south to land near San Francisco in 1579. Details are lost, and may have been deliberately kept secret.*

The first recorded encounter between the First Nations people and Europeans occurred in 1774, when a Spanish expedition led by Juan Pérez, with Esteban Martínez as second-in-command, traded with the Haida off the Queen Charlotte Islands. They did not land because their ship, the *Santiago*, was not suitable for inshore exploration. On their return, they met local people off Hesquiat, just south of Nootka Sound. They exchanged gifts, likely including two silver spoons which would reappear later, and carried on south without landing. Spain's policy of keeping its discoveries secret made it difficult for it to later claim possession, especially as no one actually stepped ashore.

Two further Spanish expeditions in 1775 and 1779 explored as far north as the Alaska Panhandle. Juan Francisco de la Bodega y Quadra commanded the smaller of the two vessels on both expeditions. It was partly due to this experience that he was later chosen to represent Spain in the settling of the Nootka Convention of 1792.

## CAPTAIN COOK FIRST ASHORE

The first documented European landing on what is now the British Columbia coast was made by Britain's Captain James Cook. In 1778, Cook, who was on his last great voyage round the world, spent a month in Nootka Sound repairing his two ships, the thirty-six-metre *HMS Resolution* and the thirty-one-metre *HMS Discovery*.

The purpose of Cook's voyage was to find a northern passage from the Pacific to the Atlantic, thus giving Britain faster access to the fabulous silks and spices of the Orient. The Spanish were known to be in the area, but the Admiralty instructed Cook not to visit any Spanish dominions except in an emergency and "not to lose any time in exploring"[1] except for getting "wood and water."[2] When he reached 65° north latitude (near today's Nome, Alaska) he was to "very carefully search for and explore such rivers or inlets as may appear to be of a considerable extent and pointing towards Hudsons or Baffins Bays."[3]

Cook's voyages were the equivalent of today's space shots. The 113 men on the *Discovery* and the 81 on the *Resolution* were carefully recruited for their expertise. The officers included a naturalist, a botanist, and an artist so that scientific discoveries could be properly identified and recorded. Many of these people, notably George Vancouver, midshipman on the *Discovery*, and William Bligh, master of the *Resolution*, went on to further distinguish themselves as explorers. Twelve years later, Captain Vancouver would return to the Pacific Northwest to chart the west coast of North America and resolve the Nootka Controversy (described later in this chapter). And Captain Bligh, after whom Bligh Island is named, later commanded the *Bounty*, whose crew mutinied in the South Pacific Ocean in 1787. He subsequently made a remarkable voyage across the south Pacific Ocean from Tonga to East Timor, sailing 5,820 kilometres in an open boat with no chart and 18 loyal followers.

## COOK'S ARRIVAL AT NOOTKA

After leaving England on his third voyage, James Cook sailed south around the Cape of Good Hope, calling in at Australia and wintering in Tahiti and Hawaii. From there he proceeded to New Albion, as the uncharted Pacific Northwest was then called. Arriving in early February, he ran into such stormy weather that he named his first landfall Cape Foul Weather (now Cape Flattery). Blown offshore again, Cook spent days tacking northward at a safe distance from the treacherous coast. He completely missed the entrance to the Strait of Juan de Fuca.

By 29 March 1778, desperate for fresh water, Cook tried to enter today's Esperanza Inlet at the north end of Nootka Island but a roiling mass of water laced with rocks deterred his efforts. After naming it the Bay of Hope, he turned south into Zuciarte Channel where he anchored for the night "in 85 fathoms of water so near the shore as to reach it with a hawser."[4] (He was probably close to today's flashing red beacon at the foot of Mt. Adair on the mainland side.) In the morning, he saw unbroken forest stretching from where the branches swept the sea at high water to the mountain tops, and he crossed to what is now called Resolution Cove on Bligh Island.

## MOWACHAHT MEET COOK

As the *Resolution* and *Discovery* dropped their anchors, several large Mowachaht canoes approached, their occupants respectfully greeting the newcomers with songs, dances, and the ceremonial strewing of eagle down on the water. They thought the white men were salmon which had transformed themselves into people, and they tried to tell them to "Nootka, Itchme Nootka, Itchme." The words meant come around to the harbour. Cook misinterpreted them and, as a result, the Europeans called both the place and the people Nootka. Today, the Nootka call themselves the Nuu-chah-nulth (when describing those indigenous to the west coast of Vancouver Island,) or Mowachaht (when referring specifically to those who lived at Yuquot).

Although neither side understood the other's language, Cook and Maquinna established a relationship based on mutual respect and trading began. The Mowachaht wanted anything metal. In exchange, they offered furs, cedar clothing, dried fish, pungent fermented fish oil, and "human skulls and hands."[5] Early explorers took the latter as evidence of cannibalism, but today's anthropologists disavow this theory. Cook accepted the furs, especially those of the sea otter, whose true value was not revealed until the expedition reached China many months later. When his own fur supply ran low, Chief Maquinna sent men to other villages for more. A second village tried to trade directly with the ships, but Maquinna's forces drove them off.

*Captain James Cook was the first European to land on the British Columbia coast.*

The ships spent a month in a protected cove which Cook named Ship Cove (it is now known as Resolution Cove). Cook had the crew make a new foremast and mizzen for the *Resolution* from a majestic Douglas fir. He also had the sailors brew beer from Sitka spruce needles and twig tips into a concentrate of hops and molasses. The resulting champagne was rationed every other day. This beer, together with clean warm clothes and regular rest (thanks to Cook's three-watch system) were part of his strategy for defeating scurvy. The disease, caused by Vitamin C deficiency, killed thousands of sailors. Although Cook received the Copley Medal from the Royal Society in 1776 for discovering the cure for scurvy, he never realised that the lemons he carried contained more Vitamin C than did the spruce tips.

## YUQUOT VISITED

While the crew was repairing the ship, Cook visited Yuquot. When he arrived, there were no totem poles like the one lying on the ground there now; instead, there was a row of big square houses built of horizontal planks about twelve metres long. Inside one of the largest houses, two immense carved figures were displayed at the back, but there were no carvings outside. Racks of fish dried on the rafters. Extended families of up to forty people and their slaves lived in each house. Each group had a separate fire, where the women cooked by plunging hot rocks into cedar boxes filled with water. John Webber, the expedition's artist, was inspired to capture this and other similar scenes which he carried back to England and which were reproduced in Cook's journals.

The Europeans could barely abide the smells and what they perceived to be the filth of the natives. The Mowachaht thought no better of Cook's crew. Inside the Mowachaht houses, rancid fish oil, urine stored for tanning, and rotting garbage blended into a distinctive stench; on the European ships, decaying salt pork, fetid bilges and concentrated human sweat left their own impact. The Mowachaht swam in the sea daily, then anointed their bodies with fermented fish oil, re-establishing a distinct body odour. The Europeans, by contrast, seldom washed either themselves or their clothes. Stench, it seems, is a matter of perspective.

Towards the end of his stay, Cook used his ships' boats to spend a day circumnavigating Bligh Island. The Tlupana village of Hoiss was deserted, but at Cheeshish, a Muchalaht village on the north side of Hanna Channel, he received a hostile reception. The chief would not be soothed by gifts, suspicious that the white men wanted to make off with his women. This and the traditional enmity between the Mowachaht of Yuquot and the Muchalaht deterred trading.

*The publication of Captain James Cook's report of fur bartering at Nootka Sound led to a stampede to the Northwest coast of America in the 1790s.*

## MYSTERIOUS SILVER SPOONS TRADED

Before the expedition left Nootka Sound on 29 April 1778, a month after his arrival, the Mowachaht offered Cook two silver spoons in trade. Although the spoons, which are now in the Mitchell Museum in Glasgow, Scotland, have no hallmarks, they are similar to others used by the Spaniards at that time. They could have been traded up the coast from California, or they could have been exchanged between Juan Pérez and the Hesquiat, a tribe living south of the Mowachaht, four years earlier.

On leaving Nootka, Cook continued up the coast to 65° north latitude near today's Nome, Alaska, in search of the Northwest Passage. He explored Prince William Sound and Cook Inlet before returning to Hawaii, where hostile natives, realising he wasn't the god they thought he was, murdered him. His ships escaped and continued on to China where the Mowachaht sea otter pelts fetched such high prices that European traders soon flocked to Nootka Sound. Over three hundred fur-trading ships arrived between 1785 and 1825, each with its own trade cargo.

### *Nuu-Chah-Nulth People*

*The Nuu-chah-nulth people are made up of fifteen tribes on the West Coast of Vancouver Island. These people were formerly referred to as Nootka because that was what Captain Cook and the fur traders called them. When the inhabitants of Yuquot (Friendly Cove) were trying to tell Cook to "come around into the harbour," he mistakenly thought that they were referring to their home as Nootka. The new name, Nuu-chah-nulth, which means "all along the mountains," was adopted in 1980 by the council representing the Nootka tribes. Whaling from ocean-going canoes was practised by both the Nuu-chah-nulth and the Makah of Washington State (the Makah are an extension of the Nuu-chah-nulth). The three dialects spoken by the Nuu-chah-nulth have also been referred to as Nootka, and comprise one of two branches of the Wakashan language stock (the other branch is spoken by the Kwakwaka'wakw [formerly called the Kwakiutl] of northern Vancouver Island, and the adjacent mainland).*

## MAQUINNA NEARLY ASSASSINATED

The first fur-trading ship to arrive in the area was the *Harmon*, captained by James Hanna. Hanna made landfall at Nootka on 8 August 1785, after a 115-day passage from Macao. The visit was nearly fatal. A practical joker lit some gunpowder under Maquinna's seat on board the ship, and his resulting burn and loss of dignity caused the natives to attack in revenge. Fortunately for Hanna, superior fire power enabled him to escape unscathed. The channel along the north side of Bligh Island is named after him.

The year after Hanna's unfortunate encounter, James Charles Strange, an Englishman who had been employed by the East India Company but who was not sponsored by them, sailed into Nootka Sound. He, too, hoped to make his fortune with sea otter furs, but, because of the blatant slaughter there were too many pelts on the market and prices had dropped by the time he reached China. Five ships visited the area in between 1785 and 1786. Gradually, merchants spread their trade north and south. Of the 330 ships which visited the North American coast between 1785 and 1825, during which time the otter trade was destroyed, it is not known how many actually came to Nootka.

## JOHN MACKAY LIVES WITH THE MOWACHAHT

Strange, after whom the island at the mouth of Tahsis Inlet is named, was the first to refer to Yuquot as Friendly Cove. He planted a garden there and left his young surgeon, John Mackay, to spend a year in Maquinna's house and record "the manners, customs, religion and government of the Nootka."[6] Unfortunately, within three weeks of Strange's departure, Mackay offended Maquinna, who cast him out of his house and treated him like a slave until he was rescued by Captain Charles W. Barkley in June 1787. Mackay's writing materials were destroyed, so he was unable to keep a journal. However, Alexander Walker, who sailed with Strange and met Mackay afterwards, included notes of an interview with the latter in his own journal. Unlike several of his contemporaries, Mackay stated in this interview that Maquinna's people were not cannibals. He explained that the pickled human hands, which both he and Captain Cook encountered, were medicinal charms. He also may have been the first European to travel the native overland trade route from Tahsis to the mouth of the Nimpkish River on Johnstone Strait, as he told Walker of being iced in (Tahsis Inlet does not freeze).

## FRANCES BARKLEY — FIRST EUROPEAN WOMAN TO VISIT

The first European woman to visit the Pacific Northwest and Friendly Cove was Frances Barkley, a seventeen-year-old English bride on her honeymoon who was present in 1787 when her husband rescued John Mackay. Ugly, smelly people, she deemed her hosts, while the Mowachaht called her ghost woman because of her white skin and dresses. Barkley Sound was named after her husband, William, the first European to see it. For many years he was denied credit for his discovery of the Strait of Juan de Fuca because a roguish fur trader, John Meares, stole his journals and appropriated the discoveries for himself.

## MEARES' PROPERTY CLAIMS

History suggests that Meares' ambitions nearly sparked a world war between England and Spain. At the north end of Friendly Cove lies another small rocky cove, where, in 1788, Meares built the forty-ton *North West America*, the first European ship to be launched in the Pacific Northwest. He later claimed to have bought from Maquinna not only the cove but also most lands around Nootka Sound.

## FIRST SPANISH SETTLEMENT

It was word that the Russians were about to establish a settlement at Nootka Sound, not Meares' activities, which caused the Spanish to send Esteban Martínez to establish a settlement and fort at Yuquot in 1789. His instructions were to be polite but discouraging to any Russians because Spain had a treaty with them; to discredit any British claims because the silver spoons brought back by Cook proved that Spain had arrived first; and to expel any Americans.

## THE NOOTKA CONTROVERSY

Martínez arrived 3 May 1789 to find two American ships, the *Columbia* and the *Washington*, and a Portuguese ship with an English crew already trading with the Mowachaht. The Portuguese ship, the *Iphigenia Nubiana*, along with the British ships the *Princess Royal* and the *Argonaut* (which were still en route to Nootka), were financed by Meares. To prevent the East India Company from claiming his profits, Meares had his ships fly the Portuguese flag. Martínez seized the *Iphigenia Nubiana* and then ordered it to sail to Macao. It ignored the Spanish wishes and went north to trade instead. Ten days later, the *Princess Royal* arrived from Bombay. Martínez graciously permitted it to take on wood and water and depart. The day after it left, the *Argonaut*, captained by James Colnett, arrived. With twenty-eight Chinese tradesmen aboard and enough equipment to set up a fort, Colnett had instructions to establish an exclusive British fur-factory on the site Meares had used. Annoyed to find the Spaniards there first, Colnett shouted imprecations at Martínez. Martínez, afraid that Colnett would establish a rival settlement nearby, promptly seized the *Argonaut*, taking all on board as prisoners and sending them to San Blas, a Spanish naval base on the Mexican coast.

## CALLICUM'S MURDER

Callicum, one of the Mowachaht chiefs who had been friendly with the British, protested this action and refused to listen to any explanations. Martínez fired his pistol to frighten the chief while another Spaniard who thought his captain had missed his target, shot and killed Callicum. Horrified, Maquinna and his people fled to Tahsis and the outer villages on Nootka Island. When the *Princess Royal* returned to Friendly Cove shortly afterwards, Martínez seized it too.

*A painting portraying the 1789 "Spanish Insult to the British Flag." A landing party led by Martínez is shown in the dastardly act of taking an officer of the Argonaut at sword point.*

## MEARES PROTESTS

The seizure of his ships enraged Meares, and he petitioned the British parliament for compensation. He claimed that Chief Maquinna — the son of the Maquinna who greeted Captain Cook — had acknowledged British sovereignty over the whole area. With British sailors languishing in Mexican prisons and traders longing for access to the fur trade, London willingly supported Meares and accepted his accusation that Martínez himself had shot Chief Callicum. The two countries, who had been threatening each other for nearly two centuries, were on the brink of war. The incident became known as the Nootka Controversy.

## NOOTKA CONVENTION

It took three attempts to resolve the Nootka Controversy. The first agreement, the Nootka Convention, was worked out in October 1790 and was amended in 1793 and 1794. Eventually, the two countries resolved their differences and the captured British ships and crews were released. Spain agreed to pay Meares damages of $210,000, and all the Nootka lands claimed by him for Britain before the crisis were to be restored. This last provision would cause further problems because Meares' published journal did not specify what these lands were.

## GARDENS AND A FORT: THE SECOND SPANISH SETTLEMENT

In 1790, a new viceroy, Revillagigedo, sent Lieutenant Francisco de Eliza to be governor of Santa Cruz de Nutka, the Spanish name for Friendly Cove. Three warships accompanied Eliza: the *Concepción*, the *San Carlos*, and the *Princesa Real* (the captured *Princess Royal*). With him also came Lieutenant Colonel Pedro de Alberni commanding a force of hand-picked marines, the Volunteers of Catalonia. This time, the settlement was to be a year round operation with a fort, a Governor's house with room to entertain up to fifty people, nine more houses and gardens for fresh produce.

A small schooner, the *Santa Saturnina*, was assembled from the remains of two other small ships: the *Santa Gertrudis de Magna* (itself rebuilt from Meares' *North West America*) and the *Jason*, which was brought to Nootka Sound aboard Colnett's ship. The *Santa Saturnina* was sent south with the *San Carlos* to explore Barkley Sound in case this proved to be the Northwest Passage.

## MALASPINA ARRIVES

In 1791 a Spanish scientific expedition commanded by Alejandro Malaspina arrived. This expedition consisted of matching thirty-six-metre corvettes — the *Descubierta* and the *Atrevida*. They had left Spain on a world cruise but orders diverted them to an unsuccessful search for the Northwest Passage. On their way south from Alaska, they called at Nootka and completed a survey of the nearby inlets.

## CEVALLOS AND ESPINOSA EXPLORE THE INLETS

During the eight days assigned for the work, Lieutenant Ciriaco de Cevallos, after whom Zeballos is named, and Lieutenant José de Espinosa took the two ships' launches and went up Muchalat, Tlupana, Tahsis, and Zeballos inlets before heading back around the outside of Nootka Island to Santa Cruz de Nutka. As a result of their visit to Tahsis, Maquinna agreed to resume friendly relations with the Spaniards for the first time since the murder of Chief Callicum two years before.

## KENDRICK BUYS LAND

The American captains, Kendrick and Gray of the *Washington* and the *Columbia*, respectively, who had previously visited the area in 1788, returned in 1791. Kendrick obtained deeds to five tracts of land of which two, Marvinas Bay and Tahsis, were in Nootka Sound. Well into the next century, Kendrick's heirs and Gray's widow tried unsuccessfully to get the U.S. Congress to back their claims to it. This purchase, however, did have an effect on the resolution of the Nootka Convention the following year.

**_Spanish Dollars_**

*Pesos, Spanish milled dollars, and pieces of eight all referred to gold coins minted in Mexico in the eighteenth century and widely used in the Caribbean, the American colonies and the Far East. Sometimes they were stamped with an "8" because they were worth eight reals, and sometimes they were simply cut in quarters, each worth "two bits." When the Cook expedition sold its sea otter pelts in China, they sold for $120 each; but later, once the market was glutted, they sold for between $22 and $37.*

## QUADRA, THE DIPLOMAT

Today's British Columbians can be thankful that the Nootka negotiations were prolonged. In 1792, George Vancouver was sent from England to resolve the matter first hand. Meanwhile, the Spanish enthusiasm for Nootka had ebbed. In August 1789, Flores, the outgoing viceroy to Mexico, had ordered Martínez to shut down the settlement at Nootka and return to San Blas. Martínez left his posting reluctantly as the Nootka Convention was being signed half way around the world.

When Malaspina returned to San Blas in 1791, he joined Martínez in a serious talk with the viceroy about the implications of the Nootka Convention. Consequently, the Viceroy assigned his commander at San Blas, Juan Francisco de la Bodega y Quadra (an experienced naval officer who had already been on two voyages to Alaska), to replace Eliza as governor of Santa Cruz de Nutka. Quadra was of Spanish parentage, but he was born in Peru. This appointment was a testament to his ability, as this was a position which, customarily, would have been filled by an officer from Spain.

Quadra sailed north with a mandate to await the arrival of Britain's representative, Captain George Vancouver. Land claimed by Meares was to be returned, and Quadra was to persuade Vancouver to accept the Strait of Juan de Fuca as the dividing line between British and Spanish interests. Spain would thus retain the present U.S. and Mexican coasts for itself.

Quadra wanted to negotiate from a position of strength and peace, so, when he arrived at Friendly Cove in April 1792, he made a point of continuing to build friendly relations with the Nuu-chah-nulth people and the foreign traders. These friendships paid off in several ways and led to the gathering of much information about local conditions. Captain Gray and another American captain, Joseph Ingraham, who were in the area told Quadra that when they asked Maquinna if Meares had ever purchased any land in Nootka Sound, he and his chiefs answered: "No, that Captain Kendrick was the only man to whom they had ever sold any land."[7] Quadra therefore believed that Meares' land claims were false. José Mariano Moziño, a Spanish botanist-naturalist who learnt the Mowachaht language, played an important part both as a recorder *(see bibliography)* and as an interpreter.

## POTLATCH AT COOPTE

Moziño has provided us with an eye-witness account of a colourful potlatch which was held in honour of Maquinna's daughter's puberty. This ceremony was held at Coopte, a Mowachaht winter village, and took place over several days. A platform with a balcony on top of it was attached to one of the houses especially for the occasion. Both the platform and the balcony "were painted white, yellow, red, blue and black with various large figures of poor design."[8]

The daughter, aged about thirteen, was dressed in soft, shredded cedar-bark clothing. Necklaces of lustrous dentalia — small shiny, tusk-like shells — ornamented her throat. Polished copper cylinders hung from her ears. Her hair, which was parted in the middle, was tightly fastened with matching copper clasps.

By wearing dentalia necklaces, Maquinna's daughter was displaying his wealth. Strings of dentalia were used as currency and for at least 3,000 years were traded all over British Columbia and as far south as California. Dentalia shells were collected by the Ehattesaht people of Esperanza Inlet, who used an elaborate arrangement of rakes to gather the shells from the ocean depths. Locations, identified by the positions of the mountains, were a strictly kept family secret handed down from generation to generation with much ceremony.

For four days Maquinna's daughter fasted inside the house before being led out onto the balcony by her father and uncle. Maquinna formally announced that she had become a woman and gave her a new name. Afterwards, the nobles sang and danced in her honour.

As the ceremonies ended, Maquinna led his daughter to a loom in his house and told her that, as she was no longer a child, she must now take her proper place among the women. For ten months, on pain of death, she remained in seclusion, eating a limited diet of special foods and learning to perform both the traditional duties of an adult woman and the responsibilities that came with being Maquinna's heir.

## GALIANO AND VALDES SENT TO EXPLORE GEORGIA STRAIT

As well as documenting Mowachaht life, the Spaniards continued to systematically explore the area. Malaspina's expedition had been unable to complete its planned exploration in 1791, and a second voyage the following year by the *Sutil* and the *Mexicana*, under the command of Galiano and Valdes, respectively, continued the task. After taking on extra crew at Friendly Cove which they reached two weeks after Quadra had arrived, they sailed for Neah Bay and the southern Gulf Islands. On 22 June 1792, off the mouth of the Fraser River, they met Captain George Vancouver and the British vessels, the *Discovery* and the *Chatham*. Although relations between the two nations were strained, their representatives on the B.C. coast had been instructed to avoid confrontation. As the only Europeans in a foreign land, the commanders of these four ships agreed to explore the Strait of Georgia together. However, after two weeks, Vancouver left to attend to the Nootka Convention and to meet with the Spanish commandant, de la Bodega y Quadra, at Friendly Cove.

## VANCOUVER ARRIVES

Vancouver reached Friendly Cove several days ahead of Galiano and Valdes. Gun salutes were exchanged between the English ships and Quadra's Spanish fort. Ashore, Vancouver found a well-established Spanish settlement complete with storehouses, workshops, a bakery, and a hospital. Gardens flourished while cattle and goats grazed. In August 1792, Vancouver wrote: "As many officers as could be spared from the vessels with myself dined with Senor Quadra, and were gratified with a repast we had lately been little accustomed to ... a dinner of five courses, consisting of superfluity of the best provisions, served with great elegance."[9] For Vancouver and his officers, the succulent juices of roast meat, with fresh peas, carrots, and potatoes made a startling change to the weeks of salt pork and hardtack which had been the fare on board ship.

*Captain George Vancouver*

## DIPLOMATIC DOUBLE TALK

Unfortunately, the diplomatic relations did not go as well as did the social ones. Vancouver had been told on his departure from Britain that details of the lands he was to claim would be sent to him aboard the supply ship, the *Daedalus*, but the only message he received was to add Port Cox (Clayoquot) to his list of British possessions. When he approached Quadra on the matter, the latter stated that all trace of Meares' two-storey house in the cove had disappeared before the Spaniards' arrival in 1789; and he produced a sworn statement from three ships' captains to that effect. He also stated that Maquinna said he had never sold any land to Meares. As a gesture of good faith, he offered to vacate the Spanish buildings so that Vancouver could take them over — an offer which Vancouver accepted. To convince the Mowachaht that the British would continue to have the same cordial relations with them as had the Spanish, Quadra and Vancouver sailed up to Tahsis in Vancouver's yawl, taking with them a full set of the former's plates and cutlery.

## QUADRA AND VANCOUVER TAKE A TRIP TO TAHSIS

At Tahsis they met Maquinna and his daughter. As Vancouver later wrote, Maquinna's daughter had "not long before been publicly and with great ceremony proclaimed sole heiress to all his property, power and dominion. The young princess was of low stature, very plump, with a round face, and small features; her skin was clean, and being nearly white, her person, altogether, though without any pretensions to beauty, could not be considered as disagreeable."[10] (This was the young woman who was celebrated at the potlatch at Coopte, described earlier by Moziño.) They had an "excellent dinner," but

**Nootka Sound People**

*Although the Mowachaht, who lived at Yuquot (now called Friendly Cove), were the most powerful tribe in Nootka Sound, they were not the only one. The Tlupana people inhabited Tlupana Inlet, wintering in villages at Head and Nesook bays and summering at Hoiss. Sometime during the nineteenth century they were absorbed into the Mowachaht, leaving their villages abandoned. The Muchalaht inhabited Muchalat Inlet and ranged inland to Muchalat Lake, fifteen kilometres north of Gold River.*

Vancouver was unimpressed by the display of dancing which followed, even though it was led by Maquinna himself.

After exchanging gifts with Maquinna, Quadra and Vancouver spent the night anchored in a cove and returned to Yuquot the next day. On the way back, Quadra asked Vancouver to name something after both of them. Since he had just circumnavigated Vancouver Island, Vancouver decided to name it the Island of Quadra and Vancouver. After the Spanish withdrawal from the area, however, the name was shortened to Vancouver Island, and a smaller island in Georgia Strait took the name Quadra.

On their return from Tahsis, Quadra changed his mind again preferring to leave the Spanish settlement intact while the land claim was referred back to the British and Spanish governments for a decision. Vancouver agreed, and Quadra returned to San Blas to report the outcome of their negotiations.

During the next two summers, Vancouver mapped the coastline as far north as Cook Inlet in Alaska. Three times he called in at Nootka hoping to receive further instructions from Britain but none came. On his last visit, he learned of Quadra's unexpected death at San Blas. Mourning his friend, Vancouver made another trip to Tahsis. This time he explored the village, marvelling at the huge house timbers and being entertained by Maquinna (he still wasn't impressed by the dancing). He learned that Maquinna's daughter had been betrothed to the eldest son of Wickaninnish, a wealthy chief from the Tofino area.

As he set sail for Britain in 1794, Spain was deciding that it was not worthwhile to continue to maintain Santa Cruz de Nutka. Their trading interests had not developed at Nootka, they only had 740 men to occupy the entire Pacific Coast, and they could still obtain sea otter furs in California.

## SPANISH LEAVE-TAKING

On 28 March 1795, Britain's Lieutenant Thomas Pearce arrived from England to witness the end of the Spanish settlement. The fort was dismantled and the Spanish flag hauled down. Pearce raised the British flag briefly before presenting it to Maquinna with instructions to raise it whenever a foreign ship approached. He informed the Mowachaht that the British king had graciously agreed to protect them and later reported that they seemed "much pleased" about this.

Both government representatives sailed away leaving Friendly Cove once more to the Mowachaht and the continuing flow of sea merchants in quest of furs. Over the next eight years, otter populations declined and Maquinna's relationship with the "Boston men" and Europeans gradually deteriorated.

## JOHN JEWITT'S SAGA

By 1803, the Spanish gardens were reduced to a few "onions, peas and turnips." So wrote John R. Jewitt, a twenty-year-old blacksmith from Hull, England, who was describing his years as Maquinna's slave (1803–05). Jewitt with the crew of the *Boston*, came from Europe round Cape Horn to trade for furs. Captain James Salter put in to replenish his wood and water supplies at Nootka Sound, understanding that the natives here were less hostile than were those further north. Cautiously, he anchored behind an island in Marvinas Bay, more than seven km north of Friendly Cove.

Unfortunately, his care did not extend to his dealings with the Mowachaht. Days later, when Maquinna complained that a gift rifle was defective, Salter replied with insults. On 22 March 1803, Maquinna, probably responding to years of frustration attacked the ship and massacred the *Boston* crew, with the exception of blacksmith John Jewitt and sailmaker John Thompson (whom Jewitt claimed was his father in order to save him). Jewitt was ordered to run the ship up on the Friendly Cove beach, where it was looted and later burned.

Jewitt and Thompson became Maquinna's slaves, doing all the heavy chores and never knowing if their heads would become display trophies, the fate of the rest of the *Boston*'s crew. Because of Jewitt's skill with metal, Maquinna treated him well. His crafted harpoon heads were so impressive that Maquinna refused to let him make them for anyone else. Like a prized possession, Maquinna took him everywhere. They went to Tahsis for the winter months, then out to Ehatisaht on Esperanza Inlet (where a reluctant Jewitt was given a bride), then back to Tahsis, Coopte, and Yuquot.

*A Narrative of the Adventures and Sufferings of John R. Jewitt* was published in 1815, and this fascinating story was retold in seventeen published editions over the next 100 years. However, it was not until 1987 that an edition was published in B.C., complete with a summary of Jewitt's post-slavery history. Jewitt's narrative remains one of B.C.'s great adventure stories. (*See Further Reading.*)

*(Top) This drawing by C. W. Jefferys shows John Jewitt forging harpoon heads for Maquinna. A dagger made by Jewitt has survived two centuries and is displayed at the U'Mista Cultural Museum in Alert Bay, B.C. (Bottom) This drawing from Jewitt's original "Narrative" depicts the* Boston *before it was attacked.*

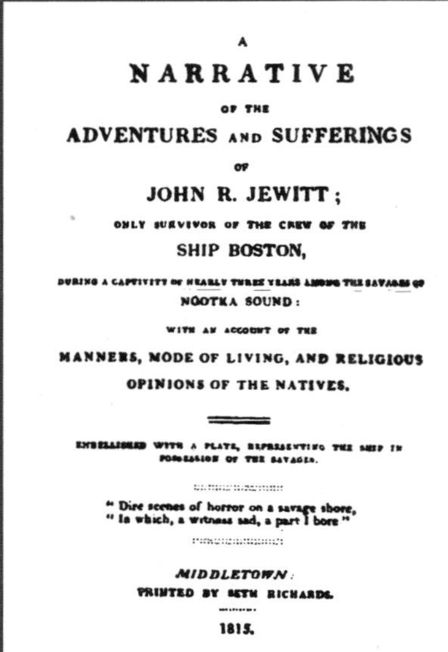

A

NARRATIVE

OF THE

ADVENTURES AND SUFFERINGS

OF

JOHN R. JEWITT;

ONLY SURVIVOR OF THE CREW OF THE

SHIP BOSTON,

DURING A CAPTIVITY OF NEARLY THREE YEARS AMONG THE SAVAGES OF

NOOTKA SOUND:

WITH AN ACCOUNT OF THE

MANNERS, MODE OF LIVING, AND RELIGIOUS

OPINIONS OF THE NATIVES.

EMBELLISHED WITH A PLATE, REPRESENTING THE SHIP IN POSSESSION OF THE SAVAGES.

" Dire scenes of horror on a savage shore,
" In which, a witness sad, a part I bore "

MIDDLETOWN:
PRINTED BY SETH RICHARDS.

1815.

*Jewitt's original title page from 1815. This narrative remains one of the most fascinating books in B.C. literature and formed the basis for* White Slaves of the Nootka, *the companion volume to this book.*

## Notes to Chapter 1

1. J.C. Beaglehole, ed., *Journals of Captain James Cook on his Voyages of Discovery,*vol 3., The Voyage of the Resolution and Discovery, 1776–1780 (Cambridge: Hakluyt Society, 1955–74), Part 2 p. ccxxi
2. J.C. Beaglehole, ed., *Journals of Captain Cook,* vol.3, Part 2 p. ccxxi
3. J.C. Beaglehole, ed., *Journals of Captain Cook,* vol.3 Part 2 p. ccxxi–ccxxii
4. J.C. Beaglehole, ed., *Journals of Captain Cook,* vol.3 Part 1 p. 295
5. J.C. Beaglehole, ed., *Journals of Captain Cook,* vol.3, Part 1 p.297
6. James Charles Strange, *James Strange's Journal and Narrative of the Commercial Exploration from Bombay to the North-West Coast of America Together with a Chart Showing the Tract of the Expedition,* (Madras: Reprinted by the Superintendent, Government Prison, 1929) p. 23.
7. Alpheus Felch, *Explorations of the North-West Coast of the United States: Report on the claims of Captains Kendrick and Gray.* (Historical Magazine, Boston Mass.,2nd series, vol. 8, September 1870, p. 158)
8. José Mariaño Mozino, *Noticias de Nutka; An Account of Nootka Sound in 1792,* translated and edited by Iris Higbie Wilson Engstrand (Vancouver, Douglas & McIntyre 1970) p. 34.
9. W. Kaye Lamb,ed. *George Vancouver, A Voyage of Discovery to the North Pacific Ocean and Round the World 1791–1795* (London, Hakluyt Society, 1984), Vol 2 p. 661.
10. W. Kaye Lamb,ed. *George Vancouver, A Voyage of Discovery,* vol 2, p. 671.

# Chapter 2

## POST JEWITT NOOTKA FROM SPOTLIGHT TO BACKDROP

Whether it was the demise of the sea otter or the popular images conjured up by readers of the Jewitt narrative, the white man's assault on Nootka slowed dramatically after 1815. For the next century and a half, only sporadic thrusts of economic interest and government issues have made Nootka newsworthy. Ironically, after being the focal point of European interest in this corner of the Pacific, the establishment of Victoria as a Hudson's Bay Company fort in the mid-19th century returned Nootka to an obscure status, a distant backdrop to the crazed hunt for gold. In a sense this rise and fall — or fall and recovery, depending on your perspective — is due to the shift from a seagoing era when Spanish and British naval captains opened up the New World. Once the development of North America became a land grab, starting in the east and moving west, across a vast continent, outposts like Nootka were protected from the European hunger to claim, tame, and harvest everything they found. Over the past 150 years, the waters and lands of Maquinna have seen some startling events and been home to some colourful characters. Yet, once visited, the beholder can only surmise that this land's true day in the sun may yet lie before us.

## A SACRED SHRINE AND CEREMONY

While at Yuquot, Jewitt must often have watched the Pacific swells crash on the long shingle beach behind the village. Here a path leads to a large fresh-water lake. An islet in the lake housed a sacred Mowachaht whaler's shrine. The shrine was kept so secret that neither Jewitt nor John Mackay, who had lived at Yuquot between 1786 and 1787, knew anything about it. It was 1817 before the French explorer, Roquefeuil, wrote the first account of this sacred place.

The chiefs performed rituals at the shrine to ensure success in the perilous whale hunt. In this hunt, crews manoeuvred their canoes close enough to the whale for the chief to harpoon it with a shell-tipped spear. Often the injured whale towed the hunters miles into the open Pacific. When the whale eventually died, one man had to dive overboard to sew the animal's mouth shut to prevent the body from sinking. Many whalers lost their prizes and their lives. Rarely was more than one whale a year brought to the village.

With the fur trade destroyed and the Boston massacre a lingering memory, the discovery of the whaler's shrine did nothing to draw more foreign visitors to Nootka Sound. By 1820 the influence of the European invaders had ebbed dramatically and life, including warfare, went on much as it had before the Europeans arrived. Both the Kyuquot to the northwest and the Muchalaht were involved in wars throughout much of the nineteenth century.

*The lake behind Friendly Cove. It was here generations of Maquinnas performed ritual ablutions in preparation for the whale hunt. The distant trees are an island which was the former site of the famous whalers shrine sold to the American Museum of Natural History in 1904 when most of the Mowachaht chiefs were away sealing in the Bering Sea.*

## MUCHALAHT WARS

The Muchalaht, unlike the other Nuu-chah-nulth people, ranged inland as well as along the inlet shores. Their sparse population made it difficult to defend such a large territory. After the trading ships disappeared in the 1820s, old hostilities were renewed. Assaults eventually came from three directions. The Mowachaht at Friendly Cove coveted their neighbour's rich Gold River salmon-spawning stream; the Nimpkish pushed down the Woss Valley trade route to the Muchalaht's inland lake settlement; and, the Hopatcisaht of Sproat Lake attacked the village of Tsaxana just north of today's Gold River. By 1860, after the wars had reduced the Muchalaht to thirty-six fighting men and their families, they retreated to their Matchlee Bay village at the head of Muchalat Inlet.

Despite the traditional animosity between the Muchalaht and the Mowachaht of Nootka Sound, there was some intermarriage. In the 1890s, one of these marriages resulted in a Muchalaht man from Matchlee Bay inheriting a Mowachaht chieftaincy. He and most of the Matchlee Village moved to Friendly Cove, though the two bands did not formally merge until 1935. Even then, the Muchalaht people clung to their separate traditions and protected their potlatch privileges.

## KYUQUOT'S LAST GREAT WAR

Though the Muchalaht lost their wars, the oral history of the First Nations people tells that the Kyuquot won theirs. When the Kyuquot talk of "the Last War," they do not mean the Second World War; they mean the war between themselves and several other Nuu-chah-nulth tribes from the south, who sent a force of 400 warriors to attack the Kyuquot summer village at Aktis. At midnight on a moonless night in 1855, 400 warriors who had been organized by the Clayoquot from the Tofino area, attacked the sleeping village. A minute before they landed, two Kyuquot returning home late yelled "Weena! Weena!" ("Strangers! Danger!") The sleepers, who had been expecting the attack for so long that they had relaxed their guard, grabbed their weapons. In the confusion, one man shot his own daughter. Crazed by grief, he then shot three Clayoquot before being killed himself. Part of the village went up in flames, survivors fleeing to the chief's house and barricading themselves in as muskets crackled all around. Kyuquot stories tell of two or three of the enemy being felled with a single shot, they were so close together. When expected reinforcements failed to show up, the disgruntled invaders retreated, blaming each other, although they had thirty-five heads and thirteen slaves to show for their attack. The Kyuquot people still talk of this event, referring to it as the "Last War."

## GUNBOATS

The Kyuquot and Muchalaht wars and others among the northern tribes, together with memories of the attacks on the *Boston* in 1803 and the *Tonquin* in Clayoquot Sound in 1811, made traders on schooners uneasy and inhibited further European settlement. These events spurred the Colonial government in Victoria to lobby the Home Office in Britain for gunboats to protect the coast. Following the Crimean War in 1859, two wooden steam gunboats, the HMS *Forward* and the HMS *Grappler*, were dispatched for this purpose. Although mainly active in the Johnstone Strait area east of Vancouver Island, they made several visits to the land of Maquinna. One of their successors, the HMS *Boxer*, sometimes transported the Roman Catholic missionaries and the Indian superintendent, though the former preferred to travel by canoe with their parishioners. The gunboats also brought liquor and supplies to everyone, along with terrible tales of what happened when villages displeased the new European masters.

The navy's flagship, the HMS *Sutlej*, whose primary purpose was to defend British interests against an American attack, used its thirty-five cannons to flatten nine Clayoquot villages and sixty-four canoes following the 1864 native attack on the *Kingfisher* at Ahousat, fifty kilometres south of Friendly Cove. However, five years later, when the *John Bright* foundered near the village of Hesquiat and the captain and crew were murdered, retribution was more focused. Two Hesquiat were convicted at a trial in Victoria and were returned to be hanged in front of their village. Hesquiat is twenty-six kilometres south of Friendly Cove.

## SMALLPOX

Although there has been speculation to the contrary, smallpox epidemics appear to have missed this area. The closest documented cases of smallpox occurred at Nitinat in 1853. Even during the terrible epidemic in March 1862, when Victoria residents evicted native people to infect communities along the Strait of Georgia and further north, the disease did not reach Nootka and Kyuquot sounds.

## MARINE SURVEYS AND MAPPING

In June of 1862, Lieutenant Philip Hankin of the survey ship, the HMS *Hecate*, and Dr. C.B. Wood of the Royal Navy were the first Europeans to explore the old native trade route across Vancouver Island from Kyuquot Sound. Disembarking the *Hecate* at Queen Cove, they travelled by canoe to Aktis, then a village of between 700 and 800 people. After a false start, they and their Kyuquot guides paddled up Tahsish Inlet and river, through the chain of lakes formed by Atluck Lake, Hustan Lake, Anutz Lake, and Nimpkish Lake to Cheslakees, a Kwakwaka'wakw village on Johnstone Strait. Then they travelled north to Fort Rupert, where they met their ship which had circumnavigated the island.

## SEALING BECAME MORE POPULAR THAN WAR

Surveys and maps made trading more attractive to Europeans. Based in Victoria, Captain William Spring and his partner, Captain Hugh McKay, operated several sealing and trading schooners (including the twenty-eight ton *Surprise*), on the coast between 1863 and 1884. The Kyuquot were the first to replace warlike activities with deep-sea voyages to California, the Bering Sea, and Japan, where they hunted seals in exchange for cash. Soon Nuchatlitz, Ehattesaht, Mowachaht, and Muchalaht men were also working for Spring and McKay, who brought trade goods for the hunters to buy with their cash. These entrepreneurs also provided the first coastal freight and passenger service from Victoria, albeit unscheduled.

*The sealing industry of Victoria was pioneered by Captain William Spring. He saw the harbour grow from a meagre group of make-do vessels to a colourful fleet of more than 100 sealing ships before 1900.*

## FATHER BRABANT BUILDS CHURCHES

One of the people who reached Nootka Sound by the Victoria service was Father Augustin Brabant, a Belgian Roman Catholic missionary. A practical man, Brabant built his own churches starting at Hesquiat in 1874 and erecting others at Kyuquot, Queen Cove, Nuchatlitz, and Friendly Cove. When neither sealing schooners nor gunboats were available, he travelled by canoe with his parishioners, visiting Nuu-chah-nulth people from Barkley Sound to the Brooks Peninsula.

The church at Friendly Cove was built in 1889 in the same cove where Meares had built his house and the *North West America* a century before. This church lasted until it was burnt down in 1954. Its replacement, which still stands, was built two years later. Father Brabant's church at Queen Cove is still occasionally used for services, but the ones at Nuchatlitz and Kyuquot are gone.

Sometimes, when he wasn't ready to build a church, Father Brabant would put up a big wooden cross. When he and Bishop Seghers from Victoria visited Kyuquot aboard the *Surprise* in 1874, they had the captain and the mate construct a twenty-four foot cross which they blessed and put up on a neighbouring island (possibly Kamils, where the Mission of St. Marc was built six years later). Sam Johnson, a Mowachaht elder, remembers as a small child, seeing a huge cross at the old village site of Ois, just before Mooyah Bay, which he says was put up by the Roman Catholic bishop.

Father Brabant not only taught the Roman Catholic faith, he also tried to teach the native peoples European niceties. He encountered much resistance when he tried to make them wear European-style clothes. The men, particularly, resented the constrictions of pants, but they eventually succumbed to the persuasion of this man of peace and his supporting gunboats. Brabant also encouraged building individual European-style houses for each man and his wife, thus breaking up the harmony and traditions of the extended family system. For several confused generations, booze became a tragic escape for a people who, traditionally, did not drink alcohol.

## CHRISTIE RESIDENTIAL SCHOOL

One of Father Brabant's dreams was to build a school for Indian children. He built the Christie Residential School at Hesquiat, which was operated from 1900 to 1971, serving the coastal villages. Brabant left the area before it became evident that, like many Indian residential schools, poor living conditions combined with rampant tuberculosis ensured that only half the children enrolled lived to enjoy the "benefits" of the education they received. Conditions were better by the time Bethine Flynn, author of *Flynn's Cove* *(see below)*, went to help in the kitchen during the last years of the school's operation. Like other Indian residential schools, it practised the unfortunate policy of punishing children who spoke their native language.

## INDIAN RESERVES

In 1881, when the West Coast Agency of Indian Affairs was set up, land was reserved for Indian use based on contemporary village and fishing sites and limited to eight hectares per family, one-eighth of the amount allocated to white settlers. This policy was arbitrary, and no treaties were signed with the tribes on the west coast of Vancouver Island.

## POTLATCHES

Both missionaries and Indian agents disapproved of the potlatch. W.H. Lomas, in a letter to I.W. Powell, the B.C. Indian commissioner, referred to potlatches as a "foolish, wasteful, demoralizing" pagan ritual. The Europeans failed to recognise it as an important social and economic system valued by all tribes along the coast. In 1885, a misguided Canadian government banned it. Only in recent years has the right of First Nation's people to pursue this ritual been restored.

*Friendly Cove 1896.*

Potlatches were major social events hosted by chiefs and their families. Feasts were prepared and non-food wealth, such as copper shields, canoes, and cedar bark clothing, were distributed in order to publicly validate some significant event like birth, marriage, or the inheritance of a traditional name, crest, or dance. In the case of Maquinna's people, guests were invited from the Hesquiat and Clayoquot to the south, the Kyuquot to the north and the Muchalaht to the east. Celebrations went on for days. At subsequent potlatches, the donors received return gifts of equal or greater value.

## REGULAR FREIGHT AND PASSENGER SERVICES BEGIN

With the Nuu-chah-nulth cowed by gunboats, restricted to reserve land, and forbidden their traditional social gatherings, an influx of European settlers slowly infiltrated the coast. Regular freight and passenger service out of Victoria started in the early 1900s with the SS *Tees*, later replaced by the *Princess Maquinna* *(see below)*. A lighthouse was built at Friendly Cove in 1910, where once the Spanish fort had stood.

## FORGER ARRESTED

In 1911, this quiet outpost experienced its first police raid. The RCMP and the FBI arrived to arrest Albert Leon, a Russian immigrant who was using a secluded two-storey cabin on the ocean side of Nootka Island to forge U.S. money, which he then distributed through a network of collaborators. The proceeds of the notes, which were found all over the U.S. and Canada, went to support the fledgling Bolshevik Revolution.

## PRINCESS MAQUINNA

Around the time of Leon's arrest, the *Tees* was replaced by the *Princess Maquinna*. This was one of the Canadian Pacific Railway's Princess boats, which once connected all the small west coast communities with Victoria. These were the *Princess Norah*, the *Princess Mary* and the *Princess Maquinna*. The *Princess Maquinna* was the most beloved, serving west coast residents from 1912 to 1952. It could carry up to 400 day passengers and sleep 100. Settlers came in on it, the sick were carried to hospitals at Port Alice and Port Alberni on it, and soldiers for two wars went out on it. Everyone got to know each other in the one big saloon, where meals of steamed salmon, new potatoes, and fresh peas and carrots were served in season. For fifty years the *Princess Maquinna* kept to its schedule in all weathers, returning to Victoria promptly at 11:00 p.m. on the 1st, 11th, and 21st of each month.

## THE CANNERIES

Among the people who travelled on the *Princess Maquinna* were the workers in the canneries. In 1897, a cannery had been built at Boca del Inferno, a kilometre north of Friendly Cove. For one brief season it canned salmon and supplied fishing boats with salt to preserve their catches. Two decades later, in 1917, an unusual influx of pilchards led to the opening of canneries at Hecate, Ceepeecee, Espinosa, Port Eliza, and Chamiss Bay as well as a new one just north of the Boca del Inferno site at Friendly Cove. The pilchards (California sardines) came in cycles, but, as Vancouver Island was the northern limit of their territory, they did not come often. The peak year of this influx was 1929, when 86,000 tons were caught; but by 1946, only 500 tons were landed, and now the fish appear to be extinct on this coast.

## EMILY CARR VISITS

The second Nootka cannery, built in 1917 by the Everett Packing Company of Washington, was located one kilometre north of its predecessor at Boco del Inferno. It soon supported a thriving community of seventy-five people. In 1929, Emily Carr, B.C.'s famous artist/writer, came to Nootka to admire the aboriginal totems. In an unpublished manuscript she wrote that the cannery's hotel "offended all my five senses."

Using the language of the day, she noted that the different ethnic groups in the community liked to remain separate. "Set back among the pines was a great raw frame building. This was where the Norwegians lived. Below them was the little Jap Village neat as a pin with little flowers and green things growing in pots." The Chinese boarding house had "tatters of derelict curtains hung at the windows and the doors and windows were tight shut." The hotel was so awful that Carr moved on to the lighthouse, which she described as "a strange wild perch" on a "nosegay of rocks, bunched with trees, spiced with wild flowers."

*Friendly Cove in the 1920s.*

## TOTEM POLE ERECTED

Emily Carr was not the only one to visit the area in 1929. Canada's governor general, Lord Willingdon, the queen's representative in Canada, also came. His visit coincided with the erection at Friendly Cove of a totem pole honouring Chief Henry Jack. This is the pole which now lies on the ground at the north end of the village.

## THE ADVENT OF THE LOGGERS

After the stock market crash of 1929, many unemployed workers came to Nootka Sound as independent loggers. They felled trees which could be pushed or pulled down to the water, gathered the logs into booms, and towed them to market in Port Alberni or Victoria.

For decades, logging on the West Coast was hindered by the difficulty of transporting logs to Victoria and Vancouver; the booms often broke up in rough seas. As a solution, in 1911, the Davis raft was developed. It consisted of logs fastened together by cables to form a thirty-seven by twenty metre raft. Logs were stacked on top of the raft until the side logs began to sink, then a steam donkey cinched wire cables tight over the top. Although this was an improvement, booms still broke up in storms. Gordon Gibson, later one of B.C.'s colourful politicians, finally solved the problem in the late 1930s with the Gibson raft — a converted rum-running schooner without its masts. It was successfully used as a log barge and opened the way for the development of West Coast logging. The remains of some

Gibson rafts can be found in the small cove just north of the Tsowwin River (these were not rum runners). Today's logging companies routinely use barges based on the Gibson raft.

*The coastal freighter* Uchuck *swings a crew member onto a floating dock as a modern logging barge lingers in the background.*

## ESPERANZA HOSPITAL

The Esperanza Hospital was founded in 1937 by Dr. Herman McLean at the urging of Percy Wills, who ran the Shantymen's Mission boat up and down the coast. (The mission was made up of a Toronto-based, self-funded group of Christian men who brought Protestant services to isolated communities throughout Canada.) Previously, the only hospital north of Tofino, was the "doll house hospital," a first-aid station in a tiny shack at the Ceepeecee Cannery, which served the whole Nootka-Kyuquot area from 1925 to 1940.

The new Esperanza Hospital brought medical care and Protestantism to the people of Esperanza Inlet, Nootka Sound, and Kyuquot. Not everyone liked its religious bias, so a community hospital soon opened at Zeballos.

Esperanza Mission on the north side of Hecate Channel, is all that remains of the Esperanza Hospital and Hotel. Built side by side, they were a strange pair. The hotel, with its well patronised liquor store, pub, and dance floor, operated from 1938 until it burned down in 1960. The land was then acquired by the mission which erected a communal dining complex on the site. The mission was run in conjunction with the Shantymen's Christian Association, (which, initially, was unable to own land). The association now runs the mission with revenue from various groups, especially those affiliated to churches and social service agencies. Other revenue comes from Louise Johnson's books about the mission: *Not Without Hope* and the *Esperanza Cookbook* (which she also edited).

Shortly after Dr. McLean retired in 1972, the hospital closed and then re-opened as a dental clinic which ran for three years. The mission also conducted activities such as the summer youth camp at Camp Ferrier (1948–1992) near Ferrer Point on the south side of Nuchatlitz Inlet.

## ZEBALLOS GOLD RUSH

The religious activities at Esperanza were in stark contrast to the secular activities of the neighbouring gold-mining town of Zeballos. "Wild and woolley Zeballos," as a contemporary T-shirt says, is now a sleepy little village of 225 people. Only fifty years ago, gold miners clutched pokes of nuggets as they drank and gambled at

*The 1935 rush to Zeballos brought another 'main street' to the Island. This time it was called Mae West Road.*

the bars and pool halls along the Mae West Road. A spotlessly clean bordello — a mile out of town — catered to other needs. Laurel and Hardy once played at the community hall, which was opened with a masked ball on Halloween night in 1938. The 1964 Alaska tidal wave lifted the hall off its foundation and left it permanently askew. Four years later, the current road was punched through, and, soon thereafter, Pacific Forest Products moved its camp from Fair Harbour to Zeballos, creating a sound economic base for the village.

Nearly 300,000 ounces of gold were mined between 1936 and 1943, with 400 men working in thirty mines having names like Privateer and Prident, White Star, and Spud Valley. The mine remains are scattered mainly on the east side of the Zeballos River. It should be noted that there were also some small iron mines.

## GORDON GIBSON BUILDS A SAWMILL

In February 1945, Gordon Gibson started building the first sawmill at Tahsis before his architect arrived. Using second-hand machinery from the old Dollarton mill in Vancouver, and an abundance of guts, drive, and ingenuity, he had the Tahsis mill producing logs for the veneer plants in Vancouver by that October. Fire destroyed the mill three years later, but Gibson was re-building before the ashes were cold.

The second mill went into operation in 1949, but conditions remained spartan. Workers stayed only as long as they could tolerate the cramped quarters, lack of dependable water and electricity, and 200 inches of winter rain. Arrivals on the weekly boat were often offset by the departures. Three years later, Gordon and his three brothers each became millionaires when they sold their operation to the Danish East Asiatic Company (EAC).

In 1954, the provincial government granted EAC a tree farm licence comprising 195,000 hectares (481,845 acres) of Nootka Sound on condition that they make long-term plans for its management. With this tenure, EAC upgraded services such as water and electricity; churches were built and schools opened. The company owned and maintained all the roads and issued its own miniature licence plates to match the 3.67-metre cars which were all that long-time manager Doug Abernethy, who had a small car himself, allowed (even Volkswagon bugs were too long). A provincially licensed booze boat made several trips a week to Tahsis.

In the 1970s, the company shed its responsibilities as town manager and applied for incorporation under the Municipal Act. Soon a rough road to the new town of Gold River opened, and the first houses were sold. Over the next two decades of road improvement, driving time was reduced from four hours to less than two.

## GOLD RIVER — A MODEL COMMUNITY

In 1965, planners and architects created an instant model community to house the families of Tahsis Company's loggers and to prepare for an influx of newcomers due to the opening of a new pulp mill. Gold River was Canada's first all-electric town, and it had underground wiring. Streets and lots were laid out for maximum privacy; picturesque street signs and hanging baskets of geraniums and lobelia adorned the lamp posts of the main thoroughfares.

However, this storybook town had its unpleasant side. Early residents like Carol and Bunty Sinclair, who came from the close-knit logging community of Beach Camp at the mouth of the Gold River (where the pulp mill was being built), found the "planned community" socially cold. Also, demand for water exceeded supply until new wells were drilled, and hydro bills were high because the green wood used in house construction needed time to dry out.

Over the next two years, 1,200 pulp mill workers and their families overwhelmed the small community of 600. Ron Foster, an ardent hiker, remembers that the newcomers were referred to somewhat derisively as "cake-eaters" because, unlike the loggers, they didn't have to work outside in the cold and dreary days of November and December. Thirty years later, common experiences have smoothed over the differences and homogenized the community of 2,200.

## PULP MILL

The Gold River pulp mill was a joint venture of the Tahsis Company and Canadian International Paper of Montreal; it was designed to utilise logs too small for export, along with wood chips from the Tahsis sawmill. Because there was no room at Tahsis and the water supply was insufficient, the mill was built on part of the A'haminaquus Indian Reserve in the Gold River estuary. In 1989, a newsprint mill was added on an adjacent site, but it closed in 1993 due to financial trouble and a shortage of fibre.

## MOWACHAHT BAND MOVES

In 1967 the federal government cut off funding for the Yuquot school, and the Gold River pulp mill opened. Although a large number of people got jobs in the pulp mill and moved to the reserve, some stayed behind on Nootka Island. With steady work the reserve residents prospered. In the ensuing thirty years, the population has increased to 160 and now there is no room on the four hectares to build additional houses. Plans have been approved to move the reserve to new land near Gold River. Of the 420 band members, 260 are now living off-reserve in Gold River, Tahsis, Courtenay, Vancouver, and other communities.

Those who stayed behind at Friendly Cove did not fare so well. "When we first came there were quite a few families still here," stated Pat Kidder of Nootka Light. "Some people would go away for the weekend and never come back. Now only the Williams Family are left," she said.

## THE WILLIAMS FAMILY REMAIN

A proud Terry Williams tells her own story. "Because we stayed after Indian Affairs cut off the funding for the school, we were told our children would never amount to anything." She and her husband Ray let the facts speak for themselves. All three children are high-school graduates. Sanford, the eldest, learned First Nations' techniques and traditions at Ksan in Hazelton, and his carvings now sell for thousands of dollars; Darryl, the middle son, is one of the best fishing guides in the area; and Sharon, the youngest, went to law school at the University of Victoria.

## TRADITIONAL VILLAGES ABANDONED IN ESPERANZA INLET

Lacking the lure of pulp-mill jobs, the bands at Ehattesaht and Nuchatlitz were less motivated to move. However, both left for the mainland when minimum enrolments were not met and their schools closed. The Ehattesaht village moved to Zeballos in 1988 and the Nuchatlitz village to Oclucje in 1987. Queen Cove is now the only inhabited native village left on Esperanza Inlet.

## LAND CLAIM

The Nuu-chah-nulth Tribal Council made a formal claim in 1980 for "all west coast lands, seas and their resources from Port Renfrew to the Brooks Peninsula." In January 1995, an "Openness protocol for the Nuu-chah-nulth treaty table" was signed by representatives of both the federal and provincial governments and the tribal council.

## CANOE REVIVAL

In 1990, two traditional canoes, the eight metre *Hlilt-he-ya-chist* and the seven metre *Hahk-kla-sis*, were built in Campbell River at the elementary school which many Ehattesaht Band children attend. These craft and others all along the coast are symbolic of a cultural revival. In David Neel's *The Great Canoes*, Victoria Wells, granddaughter of the Ehattesaht chief says: "Our culture is alive. It hasn't died, it's been in the winter phase."

## FUTURE HOPES

Today, the dark days of the twentieth century are beginning to recede for the Nuu-chah-nulth, as a vigorous new generation rejects alcohol and revives its culture. The Mowachaht are developing a flourishing tourist business at Friendly Cove, taking pride in their heritage and building their future. Rustic cabins have been built beyond the village on the lake and the seashore to house visitors. With a homeland rich in both beauty and history, Maquinna's people are poised to restore the glory of their proud past.

Today, Gold River, Nootka Sound, and the coastal inlets to the northwest remain far more remote than do most other parts of Vancouver Island. But lacking your own boat is no reason to miss out on the fun. In the next chapter, I describe one of the B.C. coast's few remaining coastal freighters, which allows landlubbers access to this adventureland.

# Chapter 3
# EXPLORING ON THE UCHUCK

All modern-day explorers who visit the land of Maquinna should consider taking at least one of the three trips offered by the historic *M.V. Uchuck III*. Water-taxi services can take you to the same places but are more expensive. Boaters harvest special rewards and enjoy the luxury of dallying at their own pace. The same pleasures and more can be enjoyed by those who do it my way — by kayak. Float planes and helicopters can extend your range but reduce your bank balance.

## M.V. UCHUCK III

The *Uchuck* is a working freight boat measuring 42 metres in length, with a beam of 7 metres and a draft of 2 metres. It travels at about 12 knots, and is powered by two 500 horsepower GM Cleveland 8-268A diesel engines. It takes up to 100 passengers to Friendly Cove, Tahsis, or even Kyuquot. The Friendly Cove trip, with all its historic elements and its intriguing church museum, is the most popular. The *Uchuck* adventure actually starts when you try to get near it. Due to cramped quarters, parking for the *Uchuck* may be some distance from the dock. Allow up to an hour from Gold River to drive the twelve kilometres, drop passengers off, and then find parking and get on board.

On days when the *Uchuck* leaves early, travellers stay the night in Gold River. "Accommodation is often booked up at the Ridgeview, the Chalet, and the Peppercorn motels so reservations

*The* M. V. Uchuck.

can be important, especially if you plan to go on the *Uchuck*," warns tall, vivacious Carol Gramlich who operates her own B&B. "I often have a full house even in winter and so does the other Carol." Both of them have converted the ground floor of their houses so that guests share a comfortable lounge, bathroom, and kitchen facilities. *(For further details, see appendices.)*

When the ship returns to Gold River, don't miss the A'haminaquus Information Centre just past the boat-launch ramp on the right. The centre is usually open when the *Uchuck* docks. In addition to buying souvenirs, ask about special events involving the Nuu-chah-nulth community, such as August house-post raising ceremonies at Friendly Cove. If the centre is closed, inquire at the band office opposite it.

## A HISTORIC SHIP

The *Uchuck III* was built in 1942 in North Bend, Oregon, as a U.S. navy minesweeper, and for four years a crew of forty saw active duty between San Francisco and Alaska. In 1951, Esson Young and George McCandless, owners of the *Uchuck II*, bought it as a stripped-down hull and scrounged parts from many sources to convert it into a freight and passenger coaster.

The *Uchuck I* and the *Uchuck II* ran freight and passenger services from Port Alberni to Barkley Sound, but, in 1960, new roads pushed Young and McCandless north. When they first started to serve Nootka Sound, there was only a limited-access logging road from Campbell River to Gold River.

In 1994, Dave Young (Esson's son) and his partner, Walter Winkler, retired and sold the *Uchuck III* to Captain Fred and Sean Mathers and Alberto Girotto, who had previously sailed on the *Lady Rose* and the *Frances Barkley* in Barkley Sound. "This is a beautifully maintained boat," said Captain Fred as he lovingly ran his hand over the polished brasswork on the bridge the day the three of them took over. As proud and experienced operators of this unique ship, I expect they will play a major role in the growth of this region as tourism expands.

**The Uchuck Dock and Drive to Gold River**

*The Uchuck docks at the government wharf, which is identified by the red paint on its railings. Nootka Air sea planes use the other side of the dock, where you may see them landing or taking off on a charter or on one of their scheduled flights to Tahsis and Kyuquot. Beyond them is the estuary of the Gold River, one of the few great wild steelhead rivers left in the province.*

*The dock is often obscured by the thick white smoke pouring out of the nearby Avenor Pulp Mill. This smoke, and a severe shortage of space, has caused the people who lived on the A'haminaquus Indian Reserve to move their village to a new site on the Tahsis Road.*

*The twelve kilometre drive into Gold River is paved all the way. Within two kilometres, the road enters the Gold River Canyon, which you can gaze into from a convenient viewpoint. Look north to catch a glimpse of white-water kayakers and rafters who have just survived the "Big Drop," a steep rapid on the river. Further on, the Lions campsite on the right has attractive riverside sites. Another two kilometres and a right-hand turn leads to Big Bend Park, a picnic site with a large sandy beach, picnic tables, and a river pool deep enough to swim in. Expect to share it with anglers and kayakers.*

*From Big Bend Park, it is only a few minutes into Gold River. As you come into town, the recreation centre on the left, with its sauna, hot tub, and swimming pool, is a good place to relax at the end of the day or before tackling the dusty logging roads.*

### On Board

Passengers have free access to a big inside cabin and an upper passenger deck with a 360° view and wooden benches to sit on. There are no private cabins. As most passengers spend a lot of time outside especially when the boat stops and the cranes hoist freight and kayakers up and down, dress in layers with something windproof on top. Don't forget sunscreen and lots of film for your camera as neither is available on board. In bad weather, sit in the combined stateroom and dining lounge. It has big windows on both sides and convenient marine charts on the tables plus a forestry map on the stern wall.

### Meals and snacks

When coming aboard early, put your order in at the galley right away for a hearty breakfast of bacon and eggs. You'll be served as soon as the crew members have had theirs. Other meals are of the home-made soup and sandwich variety, with muffins and coffee for snacks.

## FRIENDLY COVE TRIP

This comfortable day trip normally leaves at the tourist-friendly hour of 10:30 a.m. and returns before supper (call [604] 283–2325 to confirm). After a two-hour voyage in sheltered waters, you spend about ninety minutes ashore, where a Mowachaht guide will give you a tour of the village. Both the journey and the destination offer visual delights.

### Sights to See:

#### *Muchalat Inlet*

All three *Uchuck* trips go down Muchalat Inlet for the first hour or so. The steep sides of the inlet provide an example of typical West Coast coniferous rain forest. Deciduous trees need a wet summer, and most of the area's three-metre rainfall occurs in the winter. A summer visit sounds wiser with each passing word, doesn't it?

A variety of trees flourish here. Mature examples of Douglas fir, Sitka spruce, Western red cedar, and Western hemlock grow to over sixty metres, while Amabilis fir and yellow cedar are only slightly shorter. Red cedars and Douglas firs can live for 1,000 years, while the yellow cedar can live for up to 1,500 years. The inlet slopes include some old clearcuts, which are larger than the forty hectare cuts permitted today.

Looking at the quiet waters, it is hard to believe that it was once the scene of bloody battles which all but annihilated the people after whom it is named. After a tragic decade, only thirty-six Muchalaht fighting men were reported on the 1860 census compared to 150 Mowachaht men. A political marriage in the 1890s paved the way for the remaining Muchalaht to move in with their traditional enemies, the Mowachaht, and now the two bands are one.

In their heyday, the Muchalaht had small summer villages at the mouth of almost every stream on Muchalat Inlet: McCurdy Creek, Silverado Creek, Mooyah Bay, and Kleeptee Creek, but the forest has swallowed all traces of them. Larger winter villages were located at Matchlee Bay and A'haminaquus (the reserve near the *Uchuck*'s dock). Cheeshish, on Hanna Channel just beyond the mouth of Muchalat Inlet, was also a Muchalaht village.

Across the inlet from the *Uchuck*'s dock a stream comes down to a couple of trailers. These are the remains of the first logging camp in the area, Jacklah Camp, built by the Gibson Brothers in the thirties.

Travelling down the inlet on a still morning, the *Uchuck* leaves a long, straight white wake. The sun highlights small islands against the dark forest backdrop and smells of coffee and bacon waft up from the galley. Because the *Uchuck* is a working freight boat, it stops at small logging camps along the way. Mooyah Bay is usually

*Sunlight picks out three islands at the mouth of Muchalat Inlet.*

one of them, and others may include Aston Creek, Houston River, and McCurdy Creek. Anything from groceries to metal beams, huge wire spools, and even trucks are unloaded and loaded from the *Uchuck*'s two hundred-ton cargo hold at these stops.

The light beacon on the north side of the mouth of Muchalat Inlet marks Atrevida Point, named after one of the ships on Alejandro Malaspina's scientific expedition. It is a popular fishing spot. Just north of it is a large flat rock with petroglyphs.

### Zuciarte Channel and Resolution Cove

Once out of Muchalat Inlet, the *Uchuck* turns west into Zuciarte Channel between Bligh Island and the mainland. At the end of the long peninsula of Bligh Island is the cove where Captain Cook spent a month in 1778. He called it Ship Cove, but the name has now been changed to Resolution Cove. Two plaques are embedded in the rocky bluffs in the centre of the cove to commemorate the event. The *Uchuck* usually pauses here.

*White shell beaches like this one in the Spanish Pilot Group only exist at low tide.*

### Spanish Pilot Group

The southern two-thirds of Bligh Island and the group of small islands known as the Spanish Pilot Group just south of it are now a provincial park. The islands' rugged coasts conceal many nooks and crannies, and you can see the occasional flash of a white-sand beach. Today, people from Gold River and Tahsis anchor float houses here for weekend fishing trips in search of thirteen to eighteen-kilogram salmon.

The short crossing from Bligh Island to Nootka Island is subject to swells from the Pacific Ocean, but any choppiness does not last long.

*On weekends, this floathouse tucked away in an inner cove of the Spanish Pilot Group echoes with friendly laughter and tall fish tales.*

### *Friendly Cove*

On the southeast corner of Nootka Island is Friendly Cove. It was called Yuquot, place of many winds, by the 4,000 Nuu-chah-nulth who lived there before the advent of the explorers and fur traders. Its people dominated the region when Cook arrived. The hereditary Mowachaht chief of Yuquot, who now lives on the A'haminaquus Reserve near Gold River, still holds the title of Maquinna, as did his ancestor in 1778. Because of the early European activities here, Friendly Cove was one of the first four places designated a National Historic Site by the Canadian government in 1923.

*The 100-foot high light atop the crest of San Rafael Island allows the beam a range of sixteen miles and has been manned by Ed and Pat Kidder for 25 years.*

As the *Uchuck* enters the cove, you will notice a lighthouse high up on a cliff on the left, an elegant church spire which rises above a wall of brambles straight ahead and a long, low narrow dock with two houses above it on the right.

In one of the houses lives Ray Williams and his family, the only members of the band to live here year round.

Once the guns of the Spanish fort boomed across the cove from the site now occupied by the lighthouse. With 200 to 300 sport-fishing boats off the point on weekends, the Nootka Lighthouse keepers perform a crucial function which has earned them medals from the federal government. Even so, despite a flurry of protests, that same government is busy automating all the lighthouses. If time permits after the tour, climb the rocky path up to the station and sign the visitors' book. The view over the Cove and up and down the coast is spectacular.

In the late 1700s, explorers and traders came to Nootka Sound and the islands by sea. Little remains of the Spanish settlement (1789–1795), but the stained-glass windows in the church were donated by the Spanish government in its memory. The present church was built in 1956 to replace an older one which burned down. The church is now a museum for some beautiful replicas of traditional Mowachaht interior houseposts. These are similar to

*Sunlight washes the former Roman Catholic church at Friendly Cove which is now a museum.*

totem poles, but they were placed inside buildings instead of outside. They consist of ancestral figures, mainly birds, animals, and fish, carved one on top of the other to honour particular people in the community. The Jack posts on the west side, which were erected in 1993, honour the Muchalaht chief, the Maquinna posts on the east side, erected in 1994, honour the Mowachaht chief.

The raising of these houseposts in the church was accompanied by songs, chants, gift-giving and a salmon barbecue. Among the guests at the Maquinna post raising were the descendants of a nineteen-year-old Yuquot woman who had gone to San Blas in 1792 on a Spanish ship. It was quite common for young people to be invited south to learn Spanish ways. On arrival, this woman lived a life of comparative luxury as a ward of the governor and was baptized Maria de Jesus de Nuca. In the course of doing some genealogical research, one of her descendants, Geraldine Shelley from San Diego, contacted the

*Left: The stained glass depiction of Father Megin Catala preaching to the Natives is a tangible reminder of the brief Spanish era at Friendly Cove. Ironically, he made no effort to convert the Mowachaht and was only there as the chaplain to the Spanish settlement.*

*Right: Whaler figure at the base of one of the two Maquinna houseposts on display inside the church at Friendly Cove.*

Mowachaht-Muchalaht Band Office. She discovered that Elder Sam Johnson of the A'haminaquus Reserve remembered that "the sister of one of my grandmothers" had left on such a voyage. He and Chief Ambrose Maquinna had long held that their Spanish cousins would be found one day and invited Shelley and her family to attend the raising of the Maquinna house posts and participate in special family chants and dances.

Adjacent to the church is a ballfield where once the Spanish gardens grew. Every year band members camp here for two weeks of socialising and renewal. It is also an opportunity for anyone with a dispute to settle to take it to the traditional dispute-settling place, Tu-tu-quis, down among the rocks on the beach behind the church. Though little used now, in the old days the disputants would talk themselves out before the whole community, and then the elders would render judgement.

Surf from the open Pacific Ocean pounds on this beach and occasionally whales can be seen from the trail above it. The trail leads along the shore, past a modern graveyard, to a large freshwater lake where cabins can be rented and where the whaler's shrine used to be *(see Chapter 2)*.

*Descendants of 18th century cousins — Mowachaht elder, Sam Johnson, welcomes Geraldine Shelley of San Diego home. One of the Johnson's "grandmothers" was the sister of Shelley's direct ancestor, a 19-year-old Mowachaht woman, Maria de Jesus de Nuca, who went to San Blas in 1792 and married there.*

Returning from the lake, you will pass the remains of the school which closed in 1967 and then examine a large totem pole lying on the ground. This was erected in 1929 in honour of Captain Jack, chief of the combined Mowachaht-Muchalaht Band in the twenties and thirties, and the first visit to Friendly Cove by a lieutenant-governor of Canada. Ten carvers from five local bands created it, and it stood proudly until the first fall storm of 1993.

Beyond the totem pole a rocky cliff separates a small beach from the rest of the cove. It was here that Maquinna permitted Meares to build the coast's first ship, the *North West America*, and it was here that a later Maquinna permitted the Roman Catholic missionary, Father Augustin Brabant, to build the first church in 1889. This burned down in 1954, and the resident priest moved away.

Although human history dominates Friendly Cove, the visit ashore provides an opportunity to see some wildlife (of which Nootka Sound has a great variety). Look for the gleaming white heads of bald eagles atop tall trees, especially perched on dead branches. Kingfishers perch on branches near the water, waiting for small fish to surface. Pigeon guillemots and marbled murrelets dive and resurface endlessly, while black oyster catchers, sandpipers, and surfbirds flutter over the rocks at low tide. Although the sea otters

*Wolf figure on the 1929 totem pole which stood at Friendly Cove until 1993.*

*Sea otters are gregarious animals.*

were hunted to extinction by fur traders in the early 1800s, they are making a comeback in the kelp beds of the outer coast, and you might catch a glimpse of one from the trail by the ocean. Whales and seals are also occasionally seen.

The return voyage on the *Uchuck* follows the same route but uses the express lane.

***Sea Otters***

*Sea otters, who live most of their lives in the kelp beds, are a much larger and different species than are the river otters, which we also see. The sea otter has the densest fur there is. The outer guard hairs form a continuous waterproof cover for the soft underfur, which remains dry and keeps the animal warm. Constant grooming is essential to keep the outer fur from matting in clumps (which would defeat the whole system). Their loosely fitting coat can easily be pulled on to their bellies for grooming (this is often what the otters are doing when you see them floating on their backs). They seldom come ashore. sea otters use pebbles as tools to open sea urchins.*

## DAY TRIP TO TAHSIS

This is a working trip which leaves early and returns late a minimum of once per week year-round, depending on the freight traffic. It's about four hours each way, with a minimum one hour stop over. This day trip provides a unique opportunity to experience a "working day" in one of the most unique settings in North America. It is full of fabulous scenery, spectacular wildlife, and friendly people.

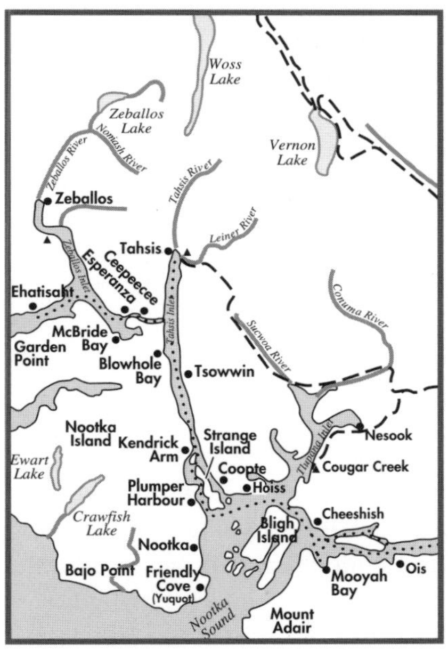


### Sights to See:

At the mouth of Muchalat Inlet about an hour from port *(see Friendly Cove Trip)*, the *Uchuck* turns north through Hanna Channel between Bligh Island and the mainland. To the right you soon see the site of the Muchalaht village, Cheeshish, where Captain Cook got a poor reception *(see Chapter 1)*. On the same side, at the mouth of Tlupana Inlet, there are often a horde of sport-fishing boats near Camel Rock. The *Uchuck* then turns west to skirt the Villaverde Islands before entering Tahsis Inlet.

The east side of Nootka Island (from Marvinas Bay just south of the mouth of Tahsis Inlet to Tahsis Narrows) as well as the south side of Esperanza Inlet have been designated as "Regionally Significant Land" by the provincial government's Commission on Resources and Environment (CORE). While this gives it less stringent protection than that enjoyed by the parkland of Bligh Island, it does give some recognition to its lovely forested slopes and wild rocky beaches. The exact rules for logging and other industrial uses of "Regionally Significant Land" are under discussion. Environmentalists would like any logging to be done with an eye to limiting its impact on the natural world; logging companies would like to be able to log as much as possible for as little as possible. High-paying jobs are at stake. Strange Island, at the entrance to Tahsis Inlet, stands as an example of 1970s logging practices; it was completely clearcut.

On the mainland opposite Strange Island is uninhabited reserve land. The gently sloping, shingle beach sometimes shows the remains of campfires. This is all that is left of Coopte, the village where the Yuquot people came in the spring on their way back from their winter quarters at Tahsis. Here they gathered herring spawn by weighting tree branches with stones, then sinking them in shallow water during the spawn. These eggs were the first new food of the year. The people considered them a great delicacy and dried them for future use. Coopte was also the site at which Maquinna held a potlatch to celebrate his daughter's puberty *(see Chapter 1)*.

**Uchuck Freight Subsidy**

*The role of a ship like the Uchuck in a region like Nootka Sound is truly appreciated when it takes needed supplies into remote locations. A government freight subsidy enables it to do this. When the Uchuck started its service to Nootka Sound in 1960 there were no roads to Tahsis or Zeballos, so the subsidies made up a large portion of the ship's budget.*

During the *Uchuck* journey up Tahsis Inlet, Nootka Island is on your left and Strange Island and the mainland are on your right. On Nootka Island, the permanent residents at the logging operations of Plumper Harbour and Kendrick Arm look forward to the regular stops. Plumper Harbour, at the entrance to Kendrick Inlet, is named after the HMS *Plumper*, a gunboat which surveyed the coast between 1857 and 1861.

Kendrick Inlet is named after John Kendrick, captain of the American ship the *Columbia*. It and the sister ship, the *Washington*, arrived at Nootka in September 1788 and traded in the area until 1791. Kendrick was a poor leader. His crews suffered from scurvy, and, on two occasions, officers deserted his command — in the Cape Verde and on the Falkland Islands. His abuse of Chief Koyah in the Queen Charlotte Islands resulted in his ship being briefly seized by the Haida. On regaining it, Kendrick shot every native in sight before he sailed away. It was behaviour like this which caused incidents like the 1803 massacre of the *Boston*'s crew in Marvinas Bay a few kilometres south of here.

Kendrick must have learned a lesson in the Charlottes because there are no stories of similar actions in Nootka Sound, though he made Marvinas Bay his headquarters. In 1791, he exchanged ten muskets with Maquinna for a deed of land to this area and obtained four other similar deeds at Tahsis, Nuchatlitz Inlet, and Clayoquot Sound. A year later, Maquinna confirmed the transaction to the American captains Gray and Ingraham, who were testifying to Quadra about Meares' activities.

At the head of Kendrick Inlet lies Bodega Island, named after Captain Juan Francisco de la Bodega y Quadra, who commanded the Spanish settlement during the summer of 1792 when Vancouver arrived. Bodega Island was clearcut in the seventies, and, opposite it, the eastern slopes of Tahsis Inlet have been logged by helicopter. This technique is very expensive but reduces the need for building and unbuilding roads. Helicopter clearcuts, though small, leave a lot of debris behind.

At Tsowwin Narrows, 3.7 kilometres further up Tahsis Inlet on the east side, deer and bear often swim across to Nootka Island. The alluvial fan formed by the Tsowwin River was once a Mowachaht village and, later, a log-sorting area.

There is a reminder of Gordon Gibson's logging activities between Tsowwin Narrows and Santiago Creek, where a wreck is marked on the chart. It is all that remains of the Number 2 Ferry which used to ply Burrard Inlet to North Vancouver. When it retired from service, Gibson brought it here for a bunkhouse, but it burned to the gunwales within two weeks of arrival.

Just over one kilometre past Santiago Creek on the Nootka Island side is Blowhole Bay, where the wind howls through a gap between the mountains. Dangerous down drafts here have resulted in two plane crashes and the loss of three lives.

On the same side and three kilometres north of Blowhole Bay is a narrow, steep-sided opening at Mozino Point. This is Tahsis Narrows at the top of Nootka Island. Beyond the narrows lies the top of Esperanza Inlet which extends west and southwest twenty-five kilometres to the Pacific Ocean. Only kayakers, dropped at this point, get to explore here. The *Uchuck* continues to the head of the inlet to Tahsis, a sawmill town with a population of 1,055. Well sheltered from the fierce winter storms which batter the coast, it used to be the winter headquarters of the Mowachaht. Each year, when they moved from Friendly Cove to Tahsis, the Mowachaht lashed two canoes together with big house planks and loaded all their gear on top. After the Europeans arrived, they learned how to rig the canoes with big square sails.

***Wolf Dance Society***

*In pre-European days, the names, songs, dances and hereditary privileges which indicated each Mowachaht person's social status were acquired during the tlõkwãna or Wolf Ritual, which was performed by a secret society of the same name and was usually held at Tahsis. Children and pre-teens were laughingly kidnapped by spirits wearing stylized wolf costumes and were hidden for several days while they learned songs and dances. Jokes were made about the negligence of parents who "let" their children be kidnapped. The word "wolf" was tabu at this time, and those who forgot were subject to further ribbing.*

*The day before the children were to display their new knowledge, the Wolf Spirits allowed them to appear on a point opposite the village. The villagers embarked in canoes to fetch them. Some parents pretending to be expert wolf catchers (though of course not mentioning the animal by name), demonstrated outlandish contraptions in support of their claims. Spirits and catchers staged a mock fight, with the Spirits trying to overturn as many canoes as possible. On the fourth attempt, the catchers were allowed to retrieve the children. Next day, after a procession through the village to show off their painted faces and special hemlock-branch apparel, each child sang, danced, or displayed his/her new names or privileges. Wealthy children sometimes attended the ceremonies in their mother's arms, and many went through the experience several times before reaching adulthood.*

From Tahsis, Mowachaht traders often portaged small canoes up the Tahsis River and over the pass to Woss Lake which they paddled down, then ran the upper Nimpkish River and paddled down Nimpkish Lake to reach the mouth of the lower Nimpkish River on the north east side of Vancouver Island. It took them eight days to get there. Precious strings of dentalia-shell money from the outer coast of Nootka Island were traded for oolichan grease from further north.

Tahsis continued to be a popular wintering place for the Mowachaht until the early twentieth century, when the opening of

Dawley's store and the cannery made it more attractive for them to remain all year round at Friendly Cove. Small groups continued to come to fish for salmon in the rivers at the head of the inlet, but otherwise, except for a few European trappers, the place was largely deserted until Gordon Gibson arrived in February 1945 to build the first sawmill.

The sawmill draws assorted commercial shipping up Tahsis Inlet — ocean freighters, tugs, and barges — all adding to the ever changing vista. After an hour ashore the return journey allows you to enjoy the effect of the afternoon sun, which reveals new perspectives on the scenic journey.

## OVERNIGHT TO KYUQUOT

By booking three to four months ahead, passengers can stay overnight with bed and breakfast at the remote fishing village of Kyuquot. As the vessel leaves at 7:00 a.m., some passengers will want to sleep the night before in Gold River. Limited camping space fills up early in the afternoon, so motels and B&Bs should be reserved well in advance.

### Sights to See:

The voyage to Kyuquot offers you an opportunity to taste a later period of history than that experienced at Friendly Cove, and you can sometimes see migrating whales and resident sea otters. The ship follows the same route as that taken on the Tahsis Day trip until it reaches Tahsis Narrows. The *Uchuck* then turns into the narrows and proceeds down Esperanza Inlet, around Tatchu Point, and north to Kyuquot. Esperanza Inlet contains a former cannery at Ceepeecee, the Esperanza Mission, several logging camps, and Flynn's Cove (made famous by Bethine Flynn's books about her idyllic life here).

The first stop after Tahsis Narrows is at Steamer Point Lodge. The property originally belonged to the nearby former Ceepeecee pilchard cannery. The small white cottage above the present dock was the home of two brothers, John and Pete Perry. They settled here when their pioneer homestead at the mouth of the Leiner River on Tahsis Inlet became too crowded after the Tahsis sawmill opened in 1947.

Sometimes the *Uchuck* also stops at Ceepeecee. Short for Canadian Packing Corporation, this is the main site of the old pilchard cannery built in 1926 near the height of the pilchard boom.

*A sport-fishing boat follows the Uchuck through Tahsis Narrows and into Esperanza Inlet.*

Part of it burned down in 1956–57, after which it became a boat repair shop on weekends.

Close by is the Esperanza Mission. The well-kept buildings on a benchland of manicured lawns are set against a backdrop of dark green forests. The concrete foundation of the old two-storey hospital is still visible, but the building itself was torn down in 1991.

A few kilometres past Esperanza on the east side of Hecate Channel is a fish farm specialising in Atlantic salmon. Although there are scores of fish farms along B.C.'s coast, many people don't like them. One reason for this is the amount of effluent produced by one such as this is equivalent to that produced by a small town; another is the potential for introducing diseases into wild salmon stocks, with disastrous consequences. On the other hand, fish farms may prove critical to sustaining a wild stock for sport-fishers. Almost 75 per cent of the B.C. salmon harvest in 1995 came from fish farms.

On the same side of the channel is Lord Waterfall on Lutes Creek. It forms a series of cascades which, at low tide, end in tidal pools fringed with bright green ulva seaweed. Watch for a bald eagle guarding his prime fishing spot. Lutes Creek is named after Del Lutes, a manager at Ceepeecee who had interests in the Zeballos mines. He also had an interest in the Zeballos bordello and, unknown to his boss, strung a telephone line along the shore between Ceepeecee and Zeballos so he could be kept informed about his business interest. William Ross Lord, after whom the waterfall was named, operated a saltery for a year at Nootka during the First World War.

*John and Pete Perry built this white cottage in 1950 after the Tahsis sawmill brought invaders to their isolated original Leiner River homestead.*

Opposite Lutes Creek is Steamer Point, which the *Uchuck* rounds as it enters the main east-west portion of Esperanza Inlet. It is named after the *Princess Maquinna* and other Canadian Pacific steamships, which provided the only means of reaching Victoria from most parts of the coast.

Two miles west of Steamer Point on the north side of the inlet lies Ehatisaht, the site of a famous and once powerful First Nations village. Here in the winter of 1804, Chief Maquinna brought captive John Jewitt to be married to the Ehattesaht chief's daughter. Now all that remains is a graveyard and a few headstones.

Here, also, stood one of the last totem poles on this coast. Sometimes called the Queen Mary pole, it was raised in 1912 in honour of Mary Jack, wife of Captain Jack of Friendly Cove. In 1985, Seabreeze Ventures, a construction company then owned by Ed Rowsell of Steamer Point Lodge, took it down and sent it to the provincial museum in Victoria. A replica, carved by Tim Paul (whose mother is buried at Ehatisaht), was erected in Zeballos in 1988 but blew down within a few weeks. There was much controversy because the elders had wanted it erected at Ehatisaht and objected to the Zeballos location; the younger members of the band wanted it to be at Zeballos so that they could have houses built there. The latter won, and their houses are just out of Zeballos on the road to Fair Harbour.

Past Ehatisaht, Espinosa Inlet opens to the north. With binoculars, you may glimpse the white cottages of Oclucje, the new home of the Nuchatlitz Band at the head of the inlet. On the opposite side of Esperanza Inlet some pretty islands with white shell beaches hide Garden Point, a popular camp spot for boaters and kayakers. Ahead at the wide mouth of a shallow bay is rocky Centre Island. The big bay contains several cabins hidden in the trees. When mink farms were in fashion, several were located here, but they were unsuccessful because the climate is not cold enough for mink.

At the west end of the bay a few small islands conceal a sheltered cove containing the ruins of the first cabin built in the area in 1914. Here the Newtons ran a store and post office long before merchants moved into either Zeballos or Tahsis. In 1956, the Flynns (a Seattle veterinarian and his wife), bought it. In *The Flying Flynns* and *Flynn's Cove* Bethine Flynn describes their life here together and her final decade here as a widow. Her many friends at Nuchatlitz, Queen Cove, Esperanza, and Christie Residential School come alive on her pages. New owners are currently rebuilding her dream.

After rounding the point at the mouth of Esperanza Inlet, the south view includes Rosa Island and the Nuchatlitz group where

*Garden Point's sheltered lagoon provides a safe haven to small boaters after an often rough crossing of Esperanza Inlet.*

fishing boats and an occasional sea otter can be seen. Several people have cottages on one of the islands and two year-round resident families have an oyster farm in a sheltered inner lagoon. The remote island comprising the Nuchatlitz Indian Reserve is unoccupied most of the time.

On the north side of Esperanza Inlet, Port Eliza is the third and last inlet to open to the north. Sometimes the *Uchuck* goes all the way up to the logging camp at its head, and sometimes it just turns into the a small inlet near the entrance where the Frank Beban logging camp has a dock. The camp itself is on the coast fifteen kilometres away near Peculiar Point. (Note: Because the *Uchuck*'s insurance policy limits the numbers of passengers it can carry outside the inlets to fourteen, this is as far as you can go without booking for the Kyuquot overnight trip.)

Across from Beban's dock is the Ehattesaht Band's Queen Cove village. Its people have always kept themselves separate from the rest of their band. On the hill above the neat white houses is one of the oldest surviving churches on the coast. It was built in the 1890s by Father Augustin Brabant, the first priest to live on the West Coast since the departure of the Spaniards. Inside the church an old dugout canoe and a big ship's bell are stored. The missionaries rang bells like this to summon the faithful to church.

*Old dugout canoe and ship's bell inside the church at Queen Cove, one of the few remaining built by Father Brabant in the late 19th century.*

## CATALA ISLAND

Catala Island at the mouth of Esperanza Inlet was first surveyed by Malaspina's 1791 expedition and was named by Galiano in 1792 after Father Magin Catala, a Franciscan monk who was chaplain at Nootka between 1792 and 1794. He is depicted in one of the stained-glass windows of the Friendly Cove church. Although the window shows him preaching to the natives, such was not his role; he was merely chaplain to the Spanish settlement.

The waters off the island are popular with sport-fishers from Tahsis, Zeballos, and other areas, as well as with the commercial fleet which often anchors behind it. The shallow depth on the north side, combined with the Pacific swells, produces a continuous surge, hence the name Rolling Roadstead. Catala, which has good camping, is now a provincial park.

*Catala Island at the mouth of Esperanza Inlet.*

Catala Island was the scene of a recent amazing dog story. In July 1994, the Victoria yacht *Jabberwocky* was anchored in the Rolling Roadstead. On board was Misty, a dog trained to swim ashore when it needed to obey a call of nature. On this occasion the family thought it was back on board and sailed away. When they discovered Misty was missing and returned there was no sign of the animal. Heartbroken, they put up a sign in the Kyuquot store. A week or so later, a group of hikers from West Coast Expeditions led by Rupert Wong was exploring the marsh at Kapoose Creek when they found a dog with bleeding paws. Misty must have swum to the mainland from Catala and run nineteen kilometres along the logging road through a big clearcut, where cougars are known to lurk. One of

Wong's group took Misty with her to Victoria for a reunion with her tearful owners.

The *Uchuck* passes between Catala and a mountainous shoreline where the shining white balls half way up Eliza Dome relay weather forecasts from the Tofino Coast Guard Radio Station. In 1862, when Captain Richards of the HMS *Hecate* was surveying the area, he named the 860-metre peak Eliza Dome in memory of Lieutenant Francisco Eliza, a Spanish naval officer who commanded the Friendly Cove settlement between 1790 and 1791.

On the other side of Peculiar Point there is a resident gray whale at the near end of Yellow Bluff Bay. The mountain behind is a scarred remnant of outdated logging practices, except for a narrow fringe of trees along the bay.

Past Catala Island, passengers on the *Uchuck* ride the often lumpy swells of the open ocean as the ship gives the shallow offshore rocks of Tatchu Point a wide berth. The cook stops serving food and everything moveable is stowed away.

Among the many tragedies at Tatchu Point is that which was experienced by Dr. Herman A. McLean of Esperanza. On 1 October, 1948, he and his fifteen-year-old son, Bruce, were returning from Kyuquot when their engine failed. "Let's stick together, Dad," cried Bruce as a huge breaker flung them into the water. Those were his last words. Green water boiled and bubbled around Dr. McLean's ears for what seemed like an eternity. Lungs bursting, he surfaced and grabbed a dark object — Bruce's lifeless body.

Seconds later he had to let go, as the waves dashed him against the rocks. Bruised and bleeding, he clawed his way up to a cleft near the top of High Rocks where cold white spray drenched him every few minutes. Hours later when the tide receded he salvaged some wet blankets, rope and cans of food from the nearby wreck of their boat and tied himself into his cleft again. After two nights and a day, a fish packer from Kyuquot rescued him.

Once round Tatchu, the *Uchuck* proceeds north along a string of tiny islands to Rugged Point. Sometimes whales are seen, and often the ship will try to get near them for its passengers' benefit. In and around the kelp beds, watch for sea otter. They are a different species from, and are larger than, the river otters with which many people confuse them. They are often seen in Nicholaye Channel at the entrance to Kyuquot Sound and just before the Mission Group.

Aktis Island, on which the Kyuquot summer village was located, and where a few people still make their homes, is part of the Mission Group of islands. However, most band members have moved across Nicholaye Channel to the Houpsitas Reserve opposite Kyuqout, which is now the main settlement.

Kyuquot is unique. Some 250 people live on nine islands, including Vancouver Island, so there are no roads. The "streets" are wide channels between the islands, although the one at the west end is too shallow for many to pass through. As everyone uses boats for transportation, all traffic signs are for boats — green and black port-hand day markers, and red-right-returning buoys. The post office, which is part of the general store on the government dock, has its mail flown in three times a week. Above the store is a cosy B&B, and there is a second one just down the trail; both are operated for *Uchuck* overnighters by the Kayra Family and both have a beautiful view.

In 1962, Esko Kayra rescued a seal pup whose mother had been shot. He bottle fed it and for over thirty years, "Miss Charlie" has been one of the family and one of the sights of Kyuquot, although the white mark Kayra painted on her forehead to prevent her being shot has faded. Harbour seals have a life expectancy of about 40 years.

Most of the European community of about 100 mainly commercial fishermen and their families live on Walters Island. *Place of Many Winds*, by Margaret Sharcott, gives an interesting account of life as a troller's wife in this area in the 1950s. It is very unfortunate that it is out of print, for it contains much useful information about anchorages and places to see in the surrounding inlets.

*The government dock and European settlement at Walter's Cove, Kyuquot.*

**Hebrides Parallel**

*As a teenager I spent many summers on the island of Iona in the Hebrides. The best part of getting there started when the M.V.* King George V *drew away from the dock on the mainland loaded with 500 tourists, all of whom were intent on seeing the holy island where St. Columba, who brought Christianity to Scotland in the Sixth century, established a cathedral and burial place of kings. After two hours of following the south coast of the Isle of Mull, the* King George *turned north into the Sound of Iona to anchor in the brilliant blue, shallow water. Small red boats operated by Iona crofters came out to ferry the passengers ashore for a 1.5–hour visit. One year the weather was so rough that only our party of three teenagers, two children, a hutch full of guinea pigs, and parcels for the islanders were allowed off. The* Uchuck*, though carrying fewer passengers than the* King George*, has much the same ambience.*

The Kyuquot people live across the bay on the Houpsitas Reserve at Walters Cove. Many of them belong to the Jules family. The big two-storey yellow house on the Houpsitas waterfront above the old dock is the home of Chris Jules, a widow who runs a year-round B&B and is reputed to cook "the best fish and chips on the coast." All three rooms have a beautiful view over the bay to Walters Island. She started her business some twenty years ago when her children began to leave home, and it kept her going after her fisherman husband was lost at sea. Three years later two of her sons drowned while gathering gooseneck barnacles. Mrs. Jules has a variety of guests — tribal council people, government workers, and tourists. The B&B pays the bills. She keeps a truck at Fair Harbour to get her groceries, and, like most residents, she has a motor boat which she uses around town. Hidden away without a sign, there is also a restaurant on the reserve which is open for lunches and dinners in the summer. The blackberry pie is popular with kayakers. Depending on local conditions, the *Uchuck* passengers may have supper here, or at a restaurant along a shoreside trail near the B&Bs, or sometimes even on the *Uchuck* itself.

In the morning, passengers are responsible for making their own breakfast from the provisions in the fridges at the B&Bs and then for re-embarking in time for an 8:00 a.m. departure. If there is freight for places in Kyuquot Sound, two or three hours may be spent delivering it before the return trip begins.

The most likely stop is Chamiss Bay on the western side of Kyuquot Sound, between Moketas and Hohoae islands. Once a Kyuquot winter village, Chamiss Bay, which still operates as a logging camp, contains the remains of a logging railway and a cannery. Sometimes the *Uchuck* goes up into a sheltered inner inlet appropriately called Fair Harbour. This is where it connects to the logging-road system leading to Zeballos and Highway 19. Another side trip is up Kashutl Inlet on the west side of Kyuquot Sound, where there used to be an old copper mine and where there was once talk of putting a road through to Port Alice.

The return route out of Kyuquot Sound passes between Union Island, sheltering the mouth of the sound and Rugged Point, whose sandy beaches are a mecca for small boaters. If the *Uchuck* has spent several hours in Kyuquot Sound, the VHF radio on board will be alive with requests from logging camps like Port Eliza and Brodick Creek wanting to know what time it will arrive. The *Uchuck* responds to all requests for pick-ups, so rarely does it go non-stop to Gold River. Once, when I was aboard, she even went in to Friendly Cove and loaded a disabled power boat. All this extra unscheduled activity can make its arrival at Gold River as late as 9:00 p.m.

The uncertainty of the schedule is one of the charms of the voyage for there is always something unexpected to anticipate. While the *Uchuck* offers an ideal way to see the shoreline, to see the hidden treats beyond it, you need to take the logging roads.

# Chapter 4
## BACKROAD JAUNTS AND PRISTINE WILDERNESS

It's only about two decades since a paved Highway 19 connected the northern part of Vancouver Island to Campbell River and points south. Prior to this, access to the north was by boat or a mysterious system of restricted-travel roads designed for large trucks carrying huge logs. The main (and many of the secondary) roads of this system are now open to everyone. Lined by forests in all stages of growth, these roads skirt towering mountains and cross over steep passes to reveal spectacular views and remote lakes. Black-tailed coastal deer love to nibble on roadside grass and black bears often shepherd their cubs across the road. It's a good place to keep the camera poised.

### THE LOGGING ROAD NETWORK

Three logging-road systems service the area:

The Tahsis Road from Gold River,

The Woss Road from Gold River,

The Zeballos and Fair Harbour Road off Highway 19.

The small communities at the end of these roads are little gems of history. Tahsis, one of the first sawmill towns on the west coast, celebrates its heritage in a small museum containing many old photographs and a model bunkhouse. Comfortable modern accommodations are available as well as some interesting short hikes or you can arrange a fishing or seaplane charter. Zeballos had a gold rush in the late 1930s, and many of the original buildings with their false fronts, are still in use. The museum has photographs and artifacts which tell the story of the gold rush. Fair Harbour, a small, enclosed inlet at the end of the Zeballos road, though no longer a permanent settlement, has a summer population of fishers in RVs and a large government dock where supplies for Kyuquot residents are winched down into small motor boats.

Highway 28, the other paved highway into the Nootka Sound area, runs due west ninety kilometres from Campbell River to Gold River. Often I choose to extend this normal ninety minute drive along the shore of Upper Campbell Lake by stopping for a short hike along the well-marked trails of 200,000-hectare Strathcona Park, a wonderful destination in itself (but outside the scope of this book). Be sure to stop at one of the pull-outs overlooking the lake before descending into the Heber River Valley. Trails lead down through the salal to narrow strips of sand or shingle beach, where, on still mornings and evenings, a loon's wild call may echo across the water. Gold River, population 2,200, is a convenient place to stop for the first night. It has a friendly shopping centre, two gas stations, three motels, several B&Bs, and a tourist bureau and a golf course.

## THE TAHSIS ROAD — ACCESS TO A REMOTE INLET

The road to Tahsis runs northwest from Highway 28 near the Gold River Travel Infocentre. The pavement ends two kilometres from the highway as the road crosses a log bridge over the Gold River to a fork. The east fork to Woss is discussed later; the west fork goes to Tahsis, paralleling the Upana River, and is a well-graded gravel road. Every year, on the first weekend in June, the "Great Walk" is held. Hikers from all over the world participate *(see Chapter 5)*.

*You don't have to be young to participate in the Great Walk, a 62.5 km annual hike from Gold River to Tahsis on the first weekend of June.*

**CLIMATE**

*Gold River*
*Average temperature: 10°C*
*Extreme temperatures:*
*Winter −19°C Summer 37°C*
*Annual precipitation: 156″*

*Tahsis*
*Average temperature: 12°C*
*Extreme temperatures:*
*Winter −20°C Summer 32°C*
*Annual precipitation: 197″*

*Driest months are June, July, and August — but bring your rain gear just in case.*

One year, along this route, old air and fuel filters combined with the dry-weather dust clogged my trusty station wagon and brought it to a standstill. Luckily, other vehicles stopped to help. Traffic is scarce, and there are no gas stations until Tahsis. Within half a kilometre of the start of the Tahsis road, drivers should be careful to take the right-hand, uphill fork, otherwise they will end up back at Gold River. The fork is marked by an easily missed sign and introduces a road that snakes back and forth between hillsides clothed in cedar, hemlock, Spanish moss, alder, and bracken. The roadside slash is prime cougar country, though you'll rarely see one. During the next ninety minutes you will cross two main watersheds drained by the Upana and Conuma rivers and the Sucwoa and Perry rivers.

After the Upana Caves turnoff (details of the caves may be found in Chapter 5), the road crests through the remains of a 1958 fire, with isolated cedar trees pointing gnarled fingers out over the creek and fireweed blazing in the green below. Serried ranks of re-growth line the road above its gravelly shoulder, and mist often steals across the mountain tops, constantly changing their shapes. Small streams run along beside the road, the crystal-clear water flowing over grey stones, while in the depths of the pools, the colour deepens to an icy dark green.

The road reaches its highest point of 305 metres after climbing the Upana River Valley past Upana Lake. At the summit is small Bull Lake. In summer, if you stop here to explore, you will see yellow water lilies edging the dark lake waters. Thrushes whistle, jays scold, a wren pours forth its soul in song, and a woodpecker drums morse code on a big tree. Ravens croak distantly. You could be a thousand miles from civilization.

*Looking down Tlupana Inlet, Bligh Island (left) and the Villaverde Islands bask in the sun. The mountains of Nootka Island slope south toward Friendly Cove in the distance.*

Twenty-six kilometres from Gold River a road branches down to Nesook Bay (eleven kilometres), and Cougar Creek (sixteen kilometres). This detour from the main Gold River-Tahsis road is worth taking for the spectacular view over the islands almost to the open Pacific, which can be seen from the top of the steep, winding hill after Nesook Bay.

Cougar Creek is a popular B.C. Forest campsite and, in the summer fishing season, is jammed with campers and R.V.s. You can drive down to the boat launch and turn, but parking will be scarce. Past Cougar Creek, the road provides views over Hanna Channel and Galiano Bay. In the future, this road is expected to reach a new boat launch at the old Muchalaht village of Cheeshish.

On the way back from Cougar Creek admire the sheer cliffs guarding the entrance to Moutcha Bay, where power boats are dwarfed by the 300-metre cliffs. In the distance to the north, 1,550-metre high Mount Alava, Stevens Peak, and Mount Bate sit like a trio of blue pyramids. Some of the trees on the forested mountains welcomed Cevallos and Espinosa in 1791, when Malaspina sent them to explore and map the inlets of Nootka Sound. Little has changed.

Back on the main Gold River-Tahsis Road, the entrance to the Conuma River Valley is marked "Archery only hunting area." In the spring, when a few hunting licences for black bear, elk, and deer are issued, the Conuma campsite, one kilometre before the Conuma Hatchery, will likely be home to bow hunters from the Campbell River Fish and Wildlife Association.

Visitors to the Conuma Hatchery are welcome until 4:00 p.m. After the first autumn rain, hatchery staff collect chum salmon eggs from the Conuma, Canton, Tlupana, and Deserted rivers. The eggs are hatched in the long, narrow, outdoor pens and nurtured before being returned to their home river.

The road rises then drops to follow along the shore of Tlupana Inlet to its head. Moutcha Bay Resort is forty-two kilometres along the Tahsis Road from Gold River. For those with R.V.s, it usually offers less crowded access to Tlupana Inlet than does Cougar Creek, but only registered guests may use the private boat launch. The road then parallels the water to the Head Bay log sort before climbing up the Sucwoa Valley. Half way up on the left is the turnoff to Tsowwin, a rough boat launch on Tahsis Inlet. The road requires four-wheel drive.

Five kilometres beyond, to the right, Three Sisters Falls, a thin ribbon of white water, cascades down the cliff. Then the road passes Malaspina and Perry lakes, where fishers cast for rainbow trout.

At fifty-seven kilometres, watch for a big Douglas fir tree on the right-hand side of the road. This is the President's Tree, a landmark beloved by Tahsis residents who know that they are nearing home when they pass it. The tree is named after Jack Christiansen, former president of Tahsis Company, who, when the road was being built, decreed that a sample big fir should be left.

Further on, the green moss of the old-growth forest drenches the B.C. Forest campsite on the Leiner River and mutes the traffic noise from the road. Campers here are lulled to sleep by the river chuckling past their tents all night.

On the journey down the Leiner River Valley, Tahsis remains hidden until the last moment. The estuary on the left, just before town, is home to the native reserve, the historic winter

**Tahsis Museum**

*The Tahsis Museum and Tourist Infocentre is on the right as you drive into town (just before the mill). Its model bunkroom depicts the only accommodation in the bad old days when there was a 200% turnover of mill workers each year.*

quarters of Maquinna. Now, most band members either live in Tahsis or in Gold River.

The village of Tahsis, which is older than Gold River, hugs the shoreline round the inlet head. It began as a company town but became independent in 1970. The main employer is still the sawmill, which is now owned by Pacific Forest Products, an absentee landlord.

Commercial services include two motels, an R.V. Park, several B&Bs, one restaurant, a dozen fishing charter companies, a museum and library, a small hospital, and a grocery and liquor store. There is no bank, but most places will accept cheques or credit cards. Tahsis is a scheduled stop for Nootka Air float planes from Gold River, which taxi up to a dock between the marina and the boat-launching ramp.

The road to Tahsis is a dead end, but you can enjoy different views on your return journey, especially the one looking out towards the mouth of Head Bay into Tlupana Inlet. The cliffs below Quadra Saddle on the left-hand side of the entrance are the other side of those ones seen from the Cougar Creek Road. Being closer to them here, their 300-metre height is more believable.

Just before the bridge over the Gold River, you can choose to go north to Muchalat Lake, Woss, Zeballos, and Fair Harbour. The Zeballos-Fair Harbour Road contains several access points to Esperanza Inlet and the Kyuquot area. You may see wildlife along the way.

*Reflections in tranquil Muchalat Lake.*

## ROAD TO WOSS — CONNECTOR TO THE NORTHERN GATEWAY

If you are starting from Gold River, the route to Woss, Zeballos, and Fair Harbour is northward via logging roads from the bridge over the Gold River. Take the right fork rather than the Tahsis road. Fifteen kilometres along the road is a beautiful campsite and boat launch on the shores of Muchalat Lake, one of the traditional homes of the Muchalaht Band. In summer, the lake is warm enough to swim in, and the trout-fishing good. In the still, early morning it is easy to picture the long houses of the old Muchalaht village coming alive again.

When the village existed, people believed that, if they showed the proper respect to the spirit world, the animals would voluntarily provide them with food and clothing. Trout from the waters of the lake and berries from around it were a welcome change in diet from the salmon of Muchalat Inlet. In winter, the Muchalaht wore snow-shoes to pursue deer and elk, sometimes stripping off the rest of their clothes to brave the snow and run unencumbered after their prey.

The road continues another fifty-five kilometres to the logging community of Woss. On the way, a detour can be taken along Vernon Lake. The campsite on Vernon Lake is popular in summer,and some people have fished there for many years. Over fifty years ago, two

*When Mowachat people ran the Nimpkish River on their way to trade at Alert Bay, they would have portaged this waterfall. Now it's left to fly fishers and bald eagles.*

trappers starved to death at the south end of the lake. They kept a diary of their torment, a tragic tale related in the Heritage House book, *B.C. Provincial Police Stories*, volume 3.

Just before Woss, at the bridge over the Nimpkish River, a trail runs beside clear, green water rippling over pink rocks. In August, endless schools of sockeye swim upstream over a series of falls and a fish ladder. Bald eagles circle overhead posing a natural hazard to the fatigued fish.

Once across the bridge, turn left into Woss and make sure you gas up, as it will be your last chance before Zeballos. Drive to Highway 19 and merge with the north bound traffic from Campbell River.

## THE NORTHERN GATEWAY TO ESPERANZA INLET AND KYUQUOT SOUND

This road is accessed off the Island Highway (Highway 19). Once on the highway going north, within a few minutes from Woss, watch for the Zeballos turnoff, which is clearly marked. This is the Northern Gateway to Esperanza Inlet and Kyuquot Sound. The former gold rush town of Zeballos is forty kilometres and Fair Harbour, a popular summer base for sport-fishers, is seventy-six kilometres from the Island Highway. Two kilometres in there is a right-hand turnoff to the Hustan Caves, and at eight kilometres in there is a right-hand turnoff to Atluk Lake and the Artlish Road (which is an active logging road and not recommended for the general public).

At ten kilometres the Zeballos-Fair Harbour Road offers a view overlooking Wolfe Lake, where you can see rocky crags worthy of a mountain goat. Trees cling to crevices, and a silver streak of water falls in a series of clefts toward the greenery of the river bed.

Further on, at thirty kilometres, a dead-end road on the left leads up to a view of Tahsis. At thirty-eight kilometres the road divides, with the right fork continuing to Fair Harbour and the left fork leading four kilometres directly into Zeballos. This community was named after Lieutenant Ciriaco de Cevallos of the Spanish Navy, who, with Lieutenant José de Espinosa, used a longboat to explore the inlets on behalf of the Malaspina Expedition in 1791.

## ZEBALLOS

Zeballos is a small town with a history of gold mining. Tourists will find gas, accommodation, and several stores one of which is just beyond the government dock, where a sign states:

"Phone for service when the store is closed." For years, the only overnight accommodation was provided by the last of the frontier hotels with its noisy bar. Now there are fishing lodges and B&Bs. The Municipal Campground down by the river is peaceful — except when black bear families come to take their share of the spawning salmon in the fall. Mason Motor Lodge, once a hospital, has spacious rooms. Mason Davis, the owner, has lived in Zeballos since the 1950s and is a good source of historical information and stories.

***Zeballos Museum***

*The Zeballos Museum, which is in a small house on the left as you enter town, has photographs and artifacts relating to the gold rush. It also features Margaret Fane, the first woman who operated a radio for an airline (1938) and one of four Canadian women licensed as a commercial flier. If you have questions, or if the museum is not open, telephone the curator, Joni Guy, at 761-4070.*

## ZEBALLOS TO FAIR HARBOUR

There are two ways out of Zeballos: one leads directly onto the Fair Harbour Road, and the other leads back to Highway 19 and Port MacNeil. To see the Zeballos River Canyon, take the road you came in on, pass the cemetery, and cross the bridge, but when your road meets the main road back to Highway 19, turn left towards Fair Harbour. Drive 3.2 kilometres further on where you will see the pink cliffs of the canyon. Park and, very carefully, climb up on the rocks overlooking the river. Look back and down at a series of waterfalls and pools with dry potholes at the side. Shortly afterwards, this road joins up with the other road out of Zeballos.

Just outside Zeballos on the Fair Harbour Road is the new home of the Ehattesaht Band, which formerly lived on Esperanza Inlet. After this, the road climbs around a log-sorting area and provides good views over Zeballos Inlet. The float houses before the point with the lighthouse constitute Rogers Tyee Lodge, a fly-in salmon lodge. As the road turns west, a four-wheel-drive road on the left heads to Rhodes Creek Park, a B.C. Forest campsite. Getting down to the waterside park is easy, but getting back up without four-wheel drive may be impossible.

One kilometre along the Fair Harbour Road, the top half of Little Espinosa Inlet appears on the right. Our road soon runs over a wooden bridge between the inlet's two halves. Because it is tidal, this narrow passage periodically becomes a raging torrent of whitewater with a one-metre drop.

Four kilometres further on, there is a turnoff to Oclucje (pronounced Ook-la-gee). This hamlet of about five houses is the home of the Nuchatlitz Band, which moved here from its island village at the mouth of Esperanza Inlet in 1987. Oclucje, less than five minutes along this side road, provides a view down Espinosa Inlet. In August, fog often gags the inlet mouth, though Espinosa itself may be alive with sunshine and a stiff breeze may be stirring up whitecaps. A dock below the village has a boat-launching ramp beside it. Those who launch here should first obtain permission to park from the villagers.

When the road crosses Kaouk Creek seventeen kilometres farther on, take the left fork and admire the emerald water flowing through a miniature grey limestone canyon. The road follows the river for another nine kilometres and then starts to cross a large, open, grassy estuary to reach our destination.

In the 1950s, Fair Harbour was a permanent logging camp, but it is now abandoned. In its place is a campsite where some people spend the summer and have done so for decades. There is usually space for transients, although it will probably be further back among the mosquitoes. Water is available about half a kilometre up the side road near the bridge. Since there are no guarantees about its purity, campers should fill water containers before leaving home.

Down by the government dock there are two boat ramps. Many of the vehicles parked at the end of the road belong either to Kyuquot residents or to boaters. There have been some instances of vandalism, and a sign on a tree gives the phone number of a towing company.

While it's fun to explore the logging roads, it's nice to have an excuse to stop and enjoy your surroundings; and fishing, whether fresh-water or salt-water, is an excellent excuse. In the following chapter, I cover it and a number of other outdoor activities.

# Chapter 5
# RECREATION AND ADVENTURING

Engaging in outdoor activities is the best way to enjoy the land of Maquinna. Many people come for the fishing: big salmon and halibut in the saltchuck, wild steelhead in the Gold River, and all kinds of salmon and trout in the crystal depths of the rivers and lakes. Tales of the "one that got away" get taller and taller.

Camping expands options and exposure to interesting places. While R.V.s make good base camps, it is the backpackers who can really experience the wilderness and wake up to the dawn chorus of birds.

Hiking options abound; many are not formally documented so local information will help. I have pinpointed a variety of trails that I have either walked or had recommended by experienced locals. I also cover caves, touring the forest, mountain biking, windsurfing, diving, golfing, and white-water adventures.

## SALT-WATER FISHING

Typical of those who come for the big ones is Len Fougere, a big, bluff, retired mill-worker from Powell River who seems to know everyone. He and his four sons have been enjoying this country for over twenty years. They launch their boat at the head of Muchalat Inlet and an hour later tie up at Critter Cove, a floating marina near the mouth of Tlupana Inlet where they have a cabin reserved.

They get up at 4:30 a.m., grab a bite, and hit the water, to try their luck at the mouth of Tlupana Inlet around Camel Rock or at Hoiss Point. Next they move to the mouth of Tahsis Inlet and if they get skunked there, they go out to the lighthouse off Friendly Cove. The guides from the famed Nootka Fish Camp often start there, and many inlet regulars simply follow them.

On the maiden voyage of their six-metre boat, Len and youngest son, Blake, felt so brave they ventured out to Beano Creek in the open Pacific where, to his great delight, Len caught a sixteen kilogram spring salmon and Blake got two eleven kilogram fish. "Man, it was rough out there," Len summarized, smiling broadly as he weighed in his fish.

Inside can be rough, too, when the afternoon wind gets up. As a result, noon finds them back at Critter Cove for a late breakfast from the restaurant at the other end of the float. In the early evening, when the wind drops, they take a short trip over to Camel Rock or up the inlet.

Len buys frozen herring at the marina. He puts it in a Rhys Davies minnow teaser — a clear plastic device where the herring's head is inserted and held in place with a toothpick. "I jam in a second toothpick beside the line," Len explains, "so I can put a bend in the herring and get the right spin on it. Without this, you will not catch fish." The hook is then slipped through the tail but protrudes enough to catch anything that takes the bait.

A cut plug is also effective. This is a frozen herring cut on a forty-five-degree angle and then attached to two hooks. If fresh herring aren't available, there are plastic imitations.

Both types of bait are attached to an eleven-metre leader and then to a silver flasher. Len likes an ABE & Al No. 1 or a Gibbs Skipper, which is finished in a synthetic silver pattern. "Before I put the bait out, I test the action close to the boat to make sure it is right," Len says. "Then I let it out twelve to eighteen metres and troll at one to two knots." Most fishing is by trolling, hardly anyone casts.

When a fish strikes, it usually runs about three times before tiring. "It is wise to put the engine in neutral and lift it up so the line doesn't get wrapped around the prop," Blake says. It can take thirty-minutes to play the fish. Len has taken one of the handles off his single-action reel so that it is easier to adjust the drag without getting his knuckles bashed when the fish runs. As the fish comes close, it rolls showing its silver belly. "This is my cue to get the net under it and lift it aboard," says Blake.

According to Len, "The best way to make sure you don't catch undersize fish is to use big lures." Halibut in the eighteen to twenty-seven kilogram range are taken with the same equipment as are salmon but they are not so plentiful.

Before putting a line in the water, consult the current edition of the *B.C. Tidal Waters Sport Fishing Guide* and check for closed areas. Popular salt-water venues are listed at the back of the book. Salt-water fishing attracts hundreds of small power boaters. Most commute to and from an R.V. on a daily basis or they stay at one of the many float camps. Charter companies provide boats, guides, and accommodation for guests who fly in or who are picked up at Gold River, Tahsis, or Cougar Creek.

Most salmon caught are in the eleven to eighteen kilogram range. Advertisers may imply that larger fish are plentiful. They are not – but you can dream, and who knows what might happen. Other species caught are halibut, red snapper, ling cod, and rock cod. An

**Fishing Lodges and Camps**

*High-end fishing lodges like Nootka Island Fishing Camp, Nu•tka• Landing Floating Resort, Rogers Tyee Lodge, and Steamer Point Lodge have package deals. They will pick you up at a specified point and pamper you with luxury accommodations, experienced guides, boats and fishing gear. If you bring your own boat, marinas like Westview in Tahsis, and Critter Cove and Moutcha Bay in Tlupana Inlet are ready to service you with gas, bait, ice, and so on. When you drive to hotels and B&Bs in Tahsis, Zeballos, and Gold River; they can arrange fishing charters for you if you are prepared to make the one-to-two-hour commute to the fishing grounds. In addition, there are a number of smaller operations (many like Galiano, Bay Lodge,are located in Tlupana Inlet), whose services and prices range widely.*

*For current lists of fishing camps, contact the village of Zeballos and the infocentres at Gold River and Tahsis. Some of the high-end lodges extend their season by offering accommodations to corporate and ecotourist groups.*

analysis of fish over eighteen kilograms weighed at Critter Cove Marina showed that favourite fishing locations were Beano Creek, Maquinna and Atrevida points, and the lighthouse.

On Esperanza Inlet, "The fishing is good almost every day of the year," says Ed Rowsell, co-owner of Steamer Point Lodge. A confident former building contractor in his mid-fifties, he knows the surrounding waters well. His fund of local stories and love of telling them attract many repeat visitors to the Lodge. "Ninety per cent of all the fish caught by guests are caught between Steamer and Mozino points," he continued. Most mornings, his guides take guests on a twenty to thirty minute run to the mouth of Esperanza Inlet. This area is less crowded than what they call "the zoo" at Friendly Cove.

Guests at the Lodge have had good catches. Rowsell tells of ten doctors who flew in from Japan accompanied by their cook. Each caught a tyee (sixteen kilogram salmon), and the cook ousted Rowsell from his big commercial kitchen in the airy Lodge to produce endless sushi and other Japanese delicacies.

## FRESH-WATER FISHING

In addition to catching fish, fishers have excellent opportunities to hear and see wildlife. Almost everyone will see a dipper, a little grey bird, easily recognised as it bobs up and down on the rocks, dives into the water for a grub, and hops back up again. Columbian black-tailed deer often come down to drink, and are sometimes chased by cougar or wolves. River otters play on muddy slides serenaded by winter wrens and watched by snowy-headed bald eagles.

Those planning to fish the lakes and streams will get *British Columbia Freshwater Fishing Regulations*, when they buy a licence. These regulations are subject to change from year to year.

### I. The Gold River

The Gold River is home to some legendary wild steelhead fishing, with peak runs in December, March through May, and September. A fifteen kilogram fish, one of the largest winter steelhead recorded on Vancouver Island, was caught here in March 1974. Recommended is a pink wet fly with a line weighted to match your rod. Steelhead will snap at anything that looks like the red flash on a competing fish. They are sea-run rainbow trout, similar to Atlantic salmon, and deserve their reputation as great fighters. Fisheries regulations specify a barbless hook, and all wild fish must be returned to the water. Only a rare hatchery fish — one without an adipose fin — may be kept. Hatchery fish are not released in the Gold River.

Barry Thornton's *Steelhead* has a detailed section on the Gold River. Good maps and practical information on the Gold River and other streams is contained in *B.C. Fishing Adventures; Vancouver Island/Lower Mainland.*

### II. Tahsis Area

River fishing is popular in the Tahsis area. Don Dwulit, a wildlife photographer and ardent fisherman, says the Tahsis River has rainbow, sea-run cutthroat, and steelhead from June to September; coho in mid-September; springs after the first September rains; and sockeye, pink, and chum in mid-September. "The Tahsis River is a small river and it is hard to work," he said. "You get one bite per pool and if you see someone else on any of the rivers around here, local ethics dictate that you go away and return two hours later." For bait, he uses spinners, imitation baits, worms, and cured roe. Very few people do any fly fishing. Dwulit wears hip-waders unless he is fishing the Conuma River where chest waders are needed. He also fishes the Leiner, Perry, Sucwoa, Canton, and Tlupana rivers.

The Gold River-Tahsis Road passes close by Malaspina and Perry lakes. Malaspina Lake contains twenty-five to thirty-centimetre

*Plump cutthroat trout lurk in pools like this while dippers; tiny dark birds, trill and bob up and down on the rocks before diving in search of aquatic larvae.*

rainbow trout. The fish in Perry Lake, which is shallow — and really just the widening of the creek — are smaller. In addition, almost every one of the many log bridges on this road spans a beautiful fresh-water fishing location. The same limestone topography which created the caves has, over the centuries, resulted in miniature canyons being carved in the grey rock by the clear green and white water.

### III. Muchalat and Vernon Lakes

Muchalat Lake is good in early summer and fall for cutthroat and rainbow trout, Dolly Varden, and Kokanee. Vernon Lake is best in spring and fall for cutthroat and rainbow trout.

### IV. Zeballos Area

The Zeballos River, which runs parallel to the road, has summer and winter steelhead, cutthroat, and fall coho. Fishing is a good excuse for a leisurely hike through the river canyon, where you may see spectacular potholes formed in the limestone.

## CAMPING AND R.V.ING

All the organized road-accessible campsites are either by a river, a lake, or the sea, which makes them very attractive. R.V.ers may need to bring generators for places like Fair Harbour, Conuma River, and Cougar Creek, where there are no plug-ins. You won't find showers, but the lakes are warm. If the popular Cougar Creek is crowded, try the privately operated Moutcha Bay Marina further along the Tahsis Road. It has its own boat launch.

Sea kayakers and canoeists will have more camping options if they travel in small groups. Only Hoiss and Catala have space for more than one or two tents. The wise ones take extra tarps to build a large comfortable shelter in which to socialize if it rains.

Backpackers, especially on the Nootka Island hike *(see below)*, will have more choice. The first time you sleep out you may hear and see small creatures performing gymnastics over the walls of your tent. It's just the mice, so make sure your food is hung up out of reach and stored in something they can't chew through. In the early morning, before anyone is stirring, you may glimpse a wolf quietly sneaking home or see paw prints in the sand.

Practice no-impact camping, and pack out all garbage. There is a list of campsites in the Appendices, including those suitable for R.V.s and large tenting groups.

## HIKING

Hikes range from walks across open grassland to bushwhacking treks through awesome old-growth forest. Respect First Nations' artifacts or graves–photograph but don't touch. The Nuu-chah-nulth want their ancestors left undisturbed, and future research could be jeopardised if even microscopic traces of your presence remain.

### I. Gold River

Note: Dusk is not a good time to be on these trails. The reason? The signs say it all: "Please Beware. Wild animals may also be on path." The only wild member of the cat family on Vancouver Island is the cougar.

**The Peppercorn Trail** beside the Gold River is a thirty to forty minute walk, one way, and features clean, pebbly beaches and good swimming holes at Peppercorn Park. Access is from the park or from Muchalat Drive, opposite the high school.

**The Heber River Trail** follows a craggy grey limestone canyon a few blocks from Matchlee Drive, providing distant glimpses of the emerald river far below (twenty minutes one way).

**The Great Walk** The Gold River bridge forms the start of the famous 62.5-kilometre *Great Walk* between Gold River and Tahsis. Held on the first Saturday in June, it attracts hikers from all over the world.

Bill Rieveley of Powell River, B.C., a small sturdy man of

***Cougar***

*The only wild cat on Vancouver Island, the cougar or mountain lion, weighs up to seventy kilograms and, though rarely seen, has attacked children in Gold River and Kyuquot. Make sure children are kept close to adults. If threatened, make yourself look big and be prepared to fight it off, even with your bare hands.*

***Participating in the Great Walk***

*Pre-registering is optional. Many people gather pledges from friends for a favourite charity collecting a fixed amount for each kilometre they complete. The Walk takes place the first Saturday in June. Book accommodation in Gold River well in advance. Campers pull in the night before and park along the dusty roadside. The Walk begins at sunrise and you can rest at each checkpoint. In Tahsis, you have free use of the showers, sauna, and pool at the recreation complex. If you bring your own sleeping bag and have no other accommodation, you may sleep in the IWA Hall and buses will return you to Gold River the following morning.*

*Pre-register by sending $30 to The Great Walk, Tahsis Lions Club, Box 430, Tahsis, B.C. V0P 1X0. You can register at the last minute, but it will cost you an extra $10.*

eighty-three, was the oldest hiker for four consecutive years. His best time was a very respectable fifteen hours and five minutes.

Participants pay thirty dollars and can register one hour before a 4:00 a.m. start. Betty Ganyo, long-time organiser of the Walk for the Tahsis Lions Club, says, "It's been going for eighteen years. In 1995, we had 340 people start and 278 finished."

Checkpoints are set up every three to five kilometres with food, drink, cornstarch and band-aids for sore feet, and chairs for sore bodies. Checkpoint No. 6, at the Conuma campsite, is the half-way mark. R.V.s with toilet facilities patrol the route, along with an ambulance. Apart from the bugs in the morning, experienced hikers say that the worst part is going down the last big hill. Only beginning hikers mind steep climbs.

Bill Rieveley agrees but adds: "Traffic on the road can be a hazard. Some drivers are considerate but others are not. There have been several twisted ankles when people had to scramble off the road to avoid being run over."

On arrival at Tahsis, participants are met by a reception committee, including the Tahsis Fire Department and its blaring sirens. Each competitor passes under the symbolic pair of burning boots at the entrance to the recreation complex, where they can also have free access to the showers, sauna, and pool. Next day, everyone is returned to Gold River on buses. One year a marathoner walked all the way to Tahsis, turned around and walked all the way back to Gold River, got in his vehicle, and then drove back to Tahsis to pick up his wife, who had hiked in one direction only. Makes a person tired just reading about it, especially since a marathoner "walks" at up to thirteen kilometres an hour.

### II. Tahsis

The students at Captain Meares School have organized a ten to fifteen minute **nature walk** behind the school to observe different plant species. Expect to see broadleaf maple, red alder, Western red cedar, Western hemlock, and Sitka spruce.

**"Bull of the Woods" Trail** At the end of town from West Bay Park, there is a twenty to thirty minute hike along the water. The trail, named after Gordon Gibson, follows the shore for a short distance, ending at several picnic sites.

**Rugged Mountain** For the more adventurous, the local All Terrain Vehicle Club has a trail along the Tahsis River up to the 1,876 metre summit of Rugged Mountain. This trail can be hiked in a day.

***Overland From Tahsis***

*When Spanish lieutenants, Espinosa and Cevallos, visited Tahsis in 1791,they documented an eight-day traverse of the overland trading route described to them by Maquinna's brother-in-law. His traders carried small canoes, packed with ceremonial copper and dentalia shell, up the Tahsis Valley for two days. Then they paddled across a round lake which opened into long narrow Woss Lake. After camping on its north shore, they cautiously nosed their canoes into the swift white water of the river. One chief, Natzape, had lost his favourite wife in this river on a previous trip. Maquinna's trading party needed another two days to reach a second lake, much colder than the first. Staying close to the shore and camping at night, Nimpkish Lake took nearly four days to traverse but the river at the end of the lake provided an easy passage to saltwater. In Johnstone Strait they sought out the villages of the Kwakwaka'wakw. The Spanish never did explore this trail.*

**First Nations' Trans-Island Trading Route** The Mowachaht may have taken John Mackay over this route in 1786–7. To trade with the Kwakwa̱ka̱'wakw, they hiked up the Tahsis River, crossed a pass to Woss Lake, paddled down it, portaged and paddled down the Nimpkish River and Lake to Johnstone Strait on the east coast of Vancouver Island. In 1791, the Mowachaht told Spaniards Espinosa and Cevallos that the journey took eight days one way.

For those in good condition, the hike from Tahsis to Woss Lake takes a day. Ed Rowsell, a partner in Steamer Point Lodge, says the hike up the Tahsis River is tougher than it was before the area was logged. He described the pass between Tahsis River and Woss Lake as "spooky," with the wind always blowing.

## III. Nootka Island

**West Side of Nootka Island** This is a beautiful hike which offers opportunities to explore remote sandy ocean beaches. Start at Friendly Cove and hike past Maquinna Point to reach the flat grasslands of the ocean coast of Nootka Island. Janice Kenyon, who spent a week backpacking the twenty-four kilometres and exploring the beaches, advises: "Take extra socks and seam-sealed raingear" as well as the usual backpacking supplies for several nights in the bush. Expect to see wolf tracks and possibly the animals themselves along with black bear, whales, and sea otters. This hike can also be reached from Kendrick Arm via Crawfish Lake. It's nicer if you can get a ride up to the lake, as the road is very rough and logging trucks are a hazard.

**Owossitsa Lake** Author Bethine Flynn says it took them two hours to bushwhack the 1.4 kilometres from Owossitsa Creek on Esperanza Inlet up to the lake. I found no obvious start to the trail and no easy way up from Port Langford on the other side. Believe me, we tried. The lake would be interesting to explore by canoe, but the portage is strictly for those who like challenges.

## IV. Zeballos

**Nomash Valley** Twelve kilometres north from Zeballos, there is a right-hand turnoff which goes up the Nomash Valley. Mason Davis, owner of Mason's Motor Lodge in Zeballos, says: "At the end of the valley, beautiful alpine meadows lead to a spectacular view 549 metres down to Tahsis. There has been talk of putting a road through but it would be very steep and might scar the mountainside." Davis is very fond of this area and loves to fish the river.

**Cevallos Lake.** Davis also recommends the hike to Cevallos Lake, which is surrounded by old-growth forest. There is little undergrowth so it is an easy walk. The lake has a tideline due to a siphoning action which begins at a certain height and keeps up until the level drops two metres. No stream flows out, and cracks in the limestone provide the drainage.

Ken Brooks at the Zeballos Post Office is a knowledgeable hiker. Many of the photographs on sale at the museum were taken by his wife, Sandy, on their numerous expeditions.

**Morod's Trails.** In the days when the mines were active, a disabled Swiss prospector, Andy Morod, cleared a number of easy trails on the west side of the river near the old iron mines. Some of these can still be followed.

### V. Kyuquot Sound

**Rugged Point.** This area is best explored by walking along the sandy beaches, listening to the pounding surf. Names like Sandstone and Jurassic points refer to the geology of the area. Hikers on the beaches or the logging roads should watch the rocks for ammonites (ridged snail shells wound in a flat circle), nautiloids (like the ammonites but without the ridges), bivalves such as mussels and clams, and belemnites (cigar-shaped shells belonging to prehistoric squid). Some sources claim that the last ice age did not cover Grassy Islet, thus enabling plant species to survive there.

**Spring Island.** A narrow trail has been hacked across the island, starting at West Coast Expeditions' camp on the north side *(see Chapter 7)*. It leads through birch groves, and across small grassy meadows. In the middle of the island, the cluster of huge cedar trees is well worth a visit. At the end of the trail open savannah (with concrete pads left from a former radar station) looks out over a series of jagged, black skerries. If you scramble down onto the pebble beaches, your boots will crunch on thousands of mussel shells irridescent in the rain, tiny clam shells with brown ridges, a few arthritic-looking scallops, and chunky little top shells. It's the sort of wild place you might find glass Japanese fishing floats after a storm. No one lives permanently on Spring Island, though West Coast Expedition's annual camp remains all summer.

## MOUNTAIN BIKING

The many remote logging roads (unconnected to the Vancouver Island highway system), make this a mountain biker's paradise provided you can reach them by boat. Before you go, find out from the logging company when and where logging trucks are not likely to be active (e.g., on Nootka Island the two separate road systems start from Plumper Harbour and Kendrick Arm, both of which have logging company personnel who could tell you when would be a good time to travel). Expect very rough terrain and take lots of spare parts.

**NOT FOUND ON VANCOUVER ISLAND**

*No poisonous snakes, grizzly bears, moose, caribou, white-tailed deer, sheep, goats, coyotes, rabbits, porcupines, skunks, bobcats, and lynx.*

## FOREST TOUR

A two-hour tour starts at the Pacific Forest Products Office in the Gold River shopping centre. Trudy Annand, who conducts the minibus tours, says: "Wear stout shoes to hike through the forest, bring a cold drink and don't forget your camera. We see spectacular views of Muchalat Lake." The half dozen hikes average ten minutes each. You should be agile enough to negotiate rough ground.

The tour visits a dry-land log-sorting site, the Pacific Forest Products Company's stands of old-growth forest, and varying stands of secondary growth. Of particular interest is the thirty-year-old Cone Bank, which supports research into forest genetics at the Pacific Company's Saanich Forestry Centre by supplying it with 1.5 million seeds each year. All the trees in the bank are numbered and mapped. They originated either from seeds or grafts on roots and represent species from all over the area.

Annand explains that a ring of old growth with its high moisture content, has been left around Gold River to function as a fire guard. In areas where old growth is slated for logging, it can only be cut in forty years when the surrounding second growth matures.

The forest industry employs thirty to forty-five per cent of the labour force here, in the pulp mill at Gold River, in the sawmill at Tahsis, and in logging operations throughout the area. Pacific Forest Products holds Tree Farm Licence (TFL) No. 19, which covers 195,000 hectares from Muchalat Inlet to Espinosa Inlet. Pacific also receives lumber from the Strathcona Timber Supply Area, which comprises Nootka Island and much of the surrounding coastal watersheds.

*Trudy Annand points out a detail of the old growth forest while conducting a tour near Gold River.*

Timber Supply Areas (TSAs) are administered by the Ministry of Forests, which calls for bids from large and small contractors for harvesting rights. When TFLs and TSAs were established, logged areas were to be scientifically replanted in order to produce a continuous supply of timber. The Annual Allowable Cut (AAC) was not supposed to exceed annual growth.

But, as more British Columbians ventured off the main highways, they saw large, ugly clear-cuts that appeared abandoned. Some reacted by calling for a ban on cutting all old-growth forests; others questioned why logging companies were cutting down more trees than they were replanting. Propaganda proliferated. To date, protests in the Nootka Sound region have been without the kind of organised civil disobedience that occurred at Clayoquot Sound.

For such violations as destroying salmon streams, the B.C. Forest Practices Code has fines ranging from \$2,000 to \$1 million per day -- \$2 million per day for repeat offenders. Stumpage fees, which the companies pay for each tree cut on Crown land, have been increased and the money dedicated to reforestation. The government claims better use will be made of the forest. However, those concerned with the future of the forests are cynical: "We've heard all of the promises before." The forests in the inlets may look peaceful but under the surface there is much uncertainty.

Another forestry tour is given by Canfor's Englewood Logging Division at Woss, and you can also go on a sawmill tour at Tahsis.

## CAVES

Seventeen kilometres from Gold River, a road on the right leads to the Upana Caves, only 100 metres from its small parking area. Here, rainwater seeping through the rock has dissolved the limestone and formed dank grottos and underground caverns, with a river running through them. A descriptive pamphlet is obtainable from the Gold River Travel Infocentre. Take it with you, as there are no signs in the caves, and only one developed trail. They are, however, relatively safe; there are no sink holes to catch the unwary. The worst hazards are slippery ground and low ceilings. Water drips everywhere, and there is an all-pervasive smell of damp earth.

Sturdy boots with rubber soles and clothing suitable for slithering through narrow, muddy passages are recommended. Helmets and lights can be rented from Joe's Hardware in Gold River. Take a sweater. The year-round temperature is 7°C (45°F).

Allow one hour for trips through the main caves. Don't disturb the crickets, spiders, or other forms of cave life, and please don't touch the delicate cave formations. Stalactites and stalagmites are almost non-existent and disappointingly small; it is the chambers themselves that are interesting, and the way the river appears and disappears.

The largest of the fifteen entrances is reached by a rock staircase which leads down to the registration book and what is called Main Cave. Proceed underground a few metres to the waterfall. The river runs under Main Cave and reappears at Resurgence Cave. Along the trail, you will find an observation platform commanding a view of the Upana River and a twelve metre waterfall. Pause a while to enjoy the rushing sound of the water. There are approximately 450 metres of cave passages for those who wish to explore them.

For a fee, Karen Griffiths of Cave Treks conducts guided tours for groups of four or more people. She provides helmets with lights and is a knowledgeable spelunker. Those who have seen *Huckleberry Finn and His Friends* will recognise some of the settings, as this is where it was filmed.

There are other cave systems in this part of Vancouver Island including the White Ridge Provincial Park caves, but, as Griffiths will tell you, the Upana Caves are the only ones that are safe to explore on your own. Do not venture into the others without experienced caving guides and proper equipment. Some who have done so have died.

The White Ridge caves with a depth of 614 metres are the deepest cave system north of Mexico. Professional spelunkers Paul and Karen Griffiths have mapped over six kilometers and fourteen caves.

## DIVING

For a different perspective, try a Scuba tour with Cee Diving of Zeballos. Cliff Lovestrom, a Professional Association of Diving Instructor (PADI), will take you to see "The Garden" in Espinosa Inlet and the box crabs in Hecate Channel. Besides Barkley Sound, The Garden is the only other place on the west coast of Vancouver Island where you may see strawberry anemones. These thumbnail-sized pink or orange anemones grow only where there is a current. Octopus, six kinds of starfish, wolf eels, red Irish lords, Puget Sound king crabs, and shipwrecks are among the other attractions.

He also takes people drift-diving in Tahsis Narrows. Delicate orange and white plumose sea anemones, sea pens, and other forms of sealife reward those who venture into the depths. "Once I saw a twelve foot six gill shark there but you can't depend on them being around," Lovestrom said. This species is common in deep waters and is rarely sighted.

The Underwater Archaeological Society of B.C. has surveyed the sea floor in Friendly Cove, and their report is available from the Vancouver Maritime Museum. Its author, Jacques Marc, says findings have been disappointingly few: "There is more conjecture than reality." In particular, there are no piles of rock ballast, which should have been found there had the *Boston* been burned in Friendly Cove as Jewitt described in his *Narrative*.

## WHITE-WATER THRILLS

Both the Gold River and the Nimpkish River are discussed in Betty Pratt-Johnson's, *Whitewater Trips for Kayakers, Canoeists and Rafters on Vancouver Island.*

The Gold River — icy cold, clear and fast — has three separate trips through limestone canyons of Grades two to five white-water, including a set of rapids which kayakers call, for obvious reasons, "Big Drop." These are two kilometres downstream from the Lions campsite. Caution: This is not an area for unaccompanied novices.

The Nimpkish River has two runs. Pratt-Johnson says that the one from Kaipit Creek could be tried by beginners, and she promises "gorgeous limestone caverns curving out over the slow dark water." The other run, on the Davie Nimpkish, is for advanced paddlers only. (This may be where Chief Natzape lost his favourite wife just before Cevallos and Espinosa visited Tahsis in 1791. The couple were on the overland trail to Fort Rupert.)

White-water paddlers who can paddle a straight line without tiring may want to take their boats on the ocean. The surf beach at Escalante just south of Nootka Sound is where Strathcona Park Lodge gives surfing lessons. Don't venture into the surf unless you've had some. Wetsuits and helmets are mandatory.

## WINDSURFING

The winds which plague small boaters during the day are a delight to windsurfers, though few are seen. Tahsis and Muchalat inlets have the same windsurfing potential as does the popular Alberni Inlet off Barkley Sound to the south.

## GOLFING

The only golf course is located at Gold River. This unique nine-hole course has two sets of tee boxes and is carved out of a natural forest. The greens are of excellent quality and the small fleet of Club Cars is popular (particularly once visitors have eyed the hilly terrain).

## NEXT YEAR?

You've been on the *Uchuck* once or twice, hiked a few trails and driven the roads. Perhaps you've also fished the creeks, gone on a forestry tour, explored the caves or been diving. If only you had a boat, even a kayak or canoe. Being free to roam the waters of Maquinna is worth learning new skills. Powerboats have their place but I've managed to survive fifteen years here on paddles alone.

THE ULTIMATE – EXPLORING BY BOAT

# Chapter 6

# WHAT BOATERS AND FISHERS NEED TO KNOW

The most interesting, and the easiest, way to explore Nootka Sound and its surrounding waters is by boat. Dense forested mountains and few roads mean that large areas can only be viewed from the water and, except for Kyuquot Sound, which is only a few kilometres from the mouth of Esperanza Inlet, all the waterways connect without being exposed to the open ocean. The majority of boats seen are trailered power boats engaged in sport-fishing. Increasing numbers are paddle craft: sea kayaks, canoes, and rowboats. Others include yachts circumnavigating Vancouver Island, trailered sailboats and commercial craft (such as large ocean freighters bound for Tahsis), the commercial fishing fleet and numerous tugs and barges hauling logs and sawdust. Last, but not least, is the *M.V. Uchuck*, the most trusted and common sight in these waters.

In this chapter and the next I describe local conditions as well as several kayak and canoe trips which I have taken.

## I. WHAT BOATERS NEED TO KNOW

### A. Launches

The only boat-launching ramp with a user fee is located near the head of Muchalat Inlet at the end of Highway 28. This is the only launch ramp approachable via paved highway from Campbell River. Other launch ramps are at Cougar Creek and Nesook on Tlupana

Inlet, Tahsis, and Tsowwin (road requires four-wheel drive) on Tahsis Inlet, Zeballos on Zeballos Inlet, Oclucje on Espinosa Inlet, and Fair Harbour on Kyuquot Sound. Overnight guests at Moutcha Bay Marina may use their private launch.

## B. Gas

Marine gas is available at six locations: Gold River (near the head of Muchalat Inlet), Critter Cove Marina (mouth of Tlupana Inlet), Moutcha Bay Marina (head of Tlupana Inlet), Westview Marina (Tahsis), Esperanza Mission, and Zeballos. Diesel is available at Gold River, Tahsis, Esperanza, Zeballos, and Kyuquot.

***VHF Radio***

*Everyone on the water communicates via VHF radio. Although Tofino Coast Guard monitors Channel 16, most local people, and the Uchuck, monitor Channel 6 and switch to another channel to talk. Since VHF works on line of sight, you can't communicate over a big hump of land. When I called the Uchuck from Plumper Harbour, neither of us could hear the other until the ship turned out of Tahsis Inlet into Kendrick Inlet. If it had been an emergency, I could have called Tofino Coast Guard Radio on Channel 16 and asked them to relay the message. They, and the weather forecasts they put out, come in clearly everywhere. Weather radio receivers work well and are much cheaper than VHFs, but of course you can't call out on them.*

*VHF radio operators need to be licensed by the federal Department of Communications. The exam is easy; just show that you know how and when to send mayday and pan pan messages properly. Keep air waves clear for three minutes after the hour and the half hour so that weak distress calls can be heard.*

*Air Nootka uses aviation VHF, which is on a different frequency than is the marine VHF. They can talk to you on marine VHF but only monitor the aviation frequencies. In an emergency, the Coast Guard can relay messages to Air Nootka or a helicopter.*

*Cell phones don't work in this area yet, though satellites are being used to bring regular phone service to Kyuquot and other outlying areas.*

## C. Repairs

There is no qualified marine mechanic in the area though, for a price, one can be brought in from Campbell River. Westview Marina at Tahsis has parts catalogues available for consultation and a daily courier service. Commercial divers are available at Gold River and Zeballos and towing service is available from Westview Towing Ltd. at Tahsis. Ceepeecee has a marine ways for boats of up to 12.5 metres *(see appendices).*

## D. Hazards

The west coast of Vancouver Island is a fantastic place to explore by boat. So little has changed that much of what you see is what the European explorers saw 200 years ago. Since many of the trees live more than 1,000 years, some are undoubtedly those seen by Cook and Vancouver. On a day when the sun warms the beaches and turns the sea a deep blue, you feel you are in heaven.

But with beauty comes danger. People will tell you that small boats shouldn't come here in certain weather, and this is true. You must remember that we are talking about the open ocean, not the sheltered waters of the Strait of Georgia or Puget Sound. Coast Guard searches are expensive and difficult and unaccompanied beginners should not be here. If you have logged about 100 nautical miles in sheltered waters and have taken a course (such as that put on by the Power Squadron), you will be ready to venture out cautiously. Some of the stories in the next chapter will show you what can happen even in the inlets.

The most frequently encountered hazard is the wind, which blows strongly in the middle of the day (just when you want to be on the water); not even urban wishfuls on their annual vacations can change this. You should plan to travel early in the morning or at dusk and to relax ashore in between (this is what you'll see the fishing guides doing).

In summer, outflow winds are a problem everywhere between about 9:00 a.m. and 4:00 p.m. By mid-morning, the air above the land has heated enough to start rising and colder air is sucked in from the sea to replace it. In hot weather, the difference between day and night temperatures produces strong winds which can whip up a froth of white-capped waves with little warning. At such times, small boats should remain in harbour or hauled up on shore. As dusk falls, the land cools and the water calms. Small boats travel safely — until the reverse process gets under way. The evening wind then springs up as warm air from the land is sucked outwards to sea. Occasionally, something disturbs the pattern and the water doesn't calm down: always be aware that this may occur. In spite of this fairly regular hazard, however, small boats can travel safely early in the morning and in the evening. Outflow winds in winter are stronger and less predictable, than are those which occur in other seasons.

If you're in a sailboat or on a windsurfing board, you may want wind — but in these waters it may be too much to handle. Some sea kayakers find rough seas exhilarating; if you're in this category, plan to wear a wetsuit, as the water is frigid.

Sea fog, which is related to the inflow/outflow winds, is bothersome in August. You'll see thick fingers of it stealing up the inlets below the mountain tops, but it dissipates quickly. In the mornings, watch for the clear blue sky trying to break through just before the fog burns off. Fog can transform a familiar landscape into the mysterious. Was it a foggy day when the First Nations storytellers told of killer whales sliding up onto the smooth rocks of Bajo Point, changing into wolves, and melting into the forest?

Sometimes, when a low pressure system lies along Vancouver Island, an "alongshore stratus surge" or fog wind can occur with little change in barometric pressure. Winds change from light easterlies to strong southerlies, often rising to gale- and storm-force. Stratus clouds, fog, and a drop in temperature accompany them. When fog approaches from the south, listen for changes to the marine forecast.

Environment Canada's *Marine Weather Manual* lists the following specific hazards:

***Tatchu Point***

Westerly waves steepen on tidal currents around Tatchu Point. Conditions are hazardous under strong winds and heavy seas.

***Nuchatlitz Inlet***

Westerly waves steepen on strong ebb-tide currents in Nuchatlitz Inlet creating confused seas.

***Nootka Sound***

Gale-force outflow winds occur in Nootka Sound during the winter.

To these, the locals add Blowhole Bay on Tahsis Inlet, where sudden cross-winds have been known to flip unsuspecting power boats. Go slow.

Listen regularly to the Tofino Coast Guard Radio weather reports on VHF or weather radio. Tatchu Point is the dividing point between two forecast areas: West Coast Vancouver Island North and West Coast Vancouver Island South.

### E. Anchorages

Most coves hold only one or two boats. It is best to practise anchoring techniques before coming out, especially stern lines to shore. Books to have on board include: Don Douglass' *Exploring Vancouver Island's West Coast*, which has detailed sketch maps of many anchorages, and *Pacific Northwest Waggoner*, which has rock by rock instructions for power and sailboats, Don Watmough's *West Coast of Vancouver Island*, which is a useful reference, especially when combined with Margaret Sharcott's *Place of Many Winds*, which focuses exclusively on the Kyuquot area. Some specific anchorage tips are:

#### *At Kyuquot*

Raft up at the dock instead of dropping your anchor amongst the underwater telephone cables and stainless steel fishing lines on the bottom in Walters Cove.

#### *At Chamiss Bay*

Tie up to the booms, as the dock is very busy.

#### *In Nootka Sound*

Anchor in Santa Gertrudis Cove or the Spanish Pilot Group rather than Resolution Cove (where Captain Cook anchored). Large boats such as Cook's feel the ocean swells less than do small boats such as yours!

#### *At the head of Esperanza Inlet*

Limited moorage is available at Steamer Point Lodge for those arriving by boat, and dinner is possible if arranged in advance (this can be done over VHF radio). In the summer, the lodge monitors its fish guides on Channel 68, but in the off season they revert to Channel 6, which is what everyone else, including the *Uchuck*, uses.

**_Favourite Anchorages_**

*Santa Gertrudis Cove*

*Just north of Friendly Cove, this quiet cove, where kingfishers chitter, is sheltered from the ocean swells which affect both Resolution and Friendly coves. W.T. Dawley operated a store here from 1898 to 1927. His account books in the provincial archives show that soup plates were popular items with the Mowachaht, who purchased them both for serving food and for potlatch gifts. Identify the rocks on the chart as you proceed slowly into the cove. The north side of Spouter Island in the Spanish Pilot Group is a good alternative.*

*Queen Cove*

*This large, sheltered anchorage at the mouth of Esperanza Inlet provides a welcome refuge from the open ocean. Its calm waters reveal lots of interesting shoreline for paddle craft explorations.*

*Nesook Bay*

*At the head of Tlupana Inlet, has good anchorage in the northeast corner under the cliffs. Moutcha Bay or Hisnet Inlet are also good nearby alternatives.*

*Dixie Cove*

*Sheltered by islands, this cove in the centre of Hohoae Island in Kyuquot Sound is highly recommended by both Douglass and* Pacific Waggoner.

*Mary Basin*

*At the head of Nuchatlitz Inlet, tuck in behind Lord Island and explore the Laurie Creek waterfall in the dinghy. Caution: the sea caves near Belmont are seldom accessible by dinghy.*

*It's also well worth calling in at the remote fishing community of Kyuquot (tie up to the dock rather than dropping an anchor over their water and telephone lines), the old gold rush town of Zeballos and the village of Tahsis. Liquor is available at both Zeballos and Tahsis but not from Kyuquot.*

# Chapter 7
## THE HIGHLIGHTS PLACES TO GO

Although this section describes trips which I myself have taken in either a sea kayak or canoe in the last fifteen years, many of the places are also accessible to other small craft. The *Uchuck* makes taking kayak and canoe trips to the Nootka Sound area very easy. It will drop you off anywhere, but it requires you to rendezvous at one of its specific stops. If you've had a season or two of paddling experience

*The* M. V. Uchuck III *prepares to swing aboard some kayakers. Sea fog blankets the inlet.*

and have some knowledge of seamanship, you'll enjoy yourself. These journeys are not recommended for unaccompanied novices. After nearly thirty years of sea kayaking, canoeing, and sailing, I can safely travel alone, though I also enjoy travelling with a group.

A key requirement to enjoy this area in small craft is a willingness to get up early in order to avoid the wind. I like to paddle at 6:00 a.m. and 9:00a.m. and possibly again from 4:00 p.m. to 7:00 p.m. if the wind drops. Here it's no hardship to get up on a beautiful sunny morning. Group size should be limited to two tents unless you plan to spend all your time at Hoiss in Nootka Sound, on Catala Island, or at Rugged Point in Kyuquot Sound.

The inconvenience of the fairly predictable wind is far outweighed by days of warm sunshine on quiet beaches, often a chorus of bird songs in the background. The still morning and evenings are magical times to paddle around rocky islets, where flocks of shorebirds shimmer. Fog, which isn't usually a problem (except perhaps on August mornings), cloaks the landscape in a soft mystery, providing many unusual photo opportunities. In this almost changeless landscape, it is easy to imagine the events of earlier times — Is that a branch or the mast of a tall ship?

## I. Bligh Island and Friendly Cove

The *Uchuck* dropped me north of Bligh Island near the Villaverde Islands. The sun was warm, and my paddle hardly rippled the fluffy white clouds reflected in the still water. Lacy curtains of cedar branches looped above the rocky shoreline as I circumnavigated Verdia and Vernacci islands. At the south end of Bligh, I landed on a horseshoe of shingle on the east side of the peninsula. I was not surprised that three other batches of paddlers came and went during my five nights at this popular campsite.

The first day, I poked in and out of all the rocky chasms and tiny brilliant white-shell beaches of the Spanish Pilot Group. Black oyster catchers screamed from rock to rock, commenting on my arrival. The day I went up Ewin Inlet, I was windbound in the cove at its head for several hours. Sheltered behind a warm rock ornamented with pink fireweed and emerald moss, I alternately swam lazily, read in the sun, and watched the eagles soar against the astonishingly blue sky. Returning, the wind provided me with a tough workout.

Next morning, gentle swells accompanied me across Cook Channel to Friendly Cove. Two hundred years of history followed me round the village, the church, and the lighthouse. In the afternoon in the warm lake behind the village, chubby Mowachaht babies and their proud parents swam with me before I paddled back at sunset.

Another day, I set out eagerly round the Clerke Peninsula and into Resolution Cove, where the swells were too much for my arthritis to let me land. So, with the wind behind me, I continued on into the bay just before Concepcion Point, where I lunched and read. Rounding San Carlos Point, the wind was against me, and it took two hours to reach the shelter of Vernacci Island.

I was intent on spending my last night at Friendly Cove. As it was foggy before I left, I set a compass course for the lighthouse, but the fog lifted when I was halfway across. After making camp, I hiked back to the village lake and, as I swam, I pictured the Maquinnas conducting their whaling rituals. I envisaged them rounding the lake in a misty dawn, alternately purifying their bodies by swimming and scrubbing them with cedar boughs. Next morning, the foghorn blasted me out of my sleeping bag at dawn. Foolishly, I then spent too much time exploring Santa Gertrudis Cove and the Saavedra Islands on my way north. As a result by the time I reached Marvinas Bay, a fierce cold wind had sprung up, whipping the sea into a white froth and pursuing me relentlessly round every point until I finally reached the safe haven of Plumper Harbour. Exhausted, I dozed in the warm sun.

While this may not happen to you, it has happened to me three times when I have paddled from Friendly Cove to Plumper Harbour. If you enjoy the exhilaration of a following sea, these conditions may be fine; but, if you are a fair weather paddler like me, explore Santa Gertrudis Cove, the Saavedra Islands, and Boca de Inferno the day before you make your quick run for Plumper Harbour.

**II. Nesook Bay to Coopte**

One still August morning, nine of us, including two toddlers and a little white dog, put in at Nesook Bay and paddled our three canoes and a kayak down Tlupana Inlet. The sun was hot as we paddled past a line of small power boats stopping to watch those netting their catch. Two of our canoes trolled buzz bombs and soon we, too, were anticipating a salmon supper.

Following the north side of the inlet past Argonaut Point, beyond Critter Cove Marina we paddled west into an unnamed bay.

At the head of this bay is an intriguing mile-long lake, which is accessible only at high tide. We wanted to explore both it and the waterfalls which spill down from a lake above it. Unfortunately, the ebb tide had transformed the entrance into a shallow, rock-spiked chute of white water, so we continued on to Hoiss.

Hoiss is a former Tlupana village which has been engulfed by forest; however, recently, it has been partly cleared out. Now an army could camp between the huge trees. The remains of several old stone walls run along the side of the clearing but do not seem to enclose anything. Other Tlupana villages were at Head Bay and Nesook and nothing of them remains. The Tlupana people have long been absorbed into the Mowachaht tribe.

No doubt Tlupana children once played on the sandy beach below the Hoiss campsite. Ours did too, while the adults set up camp and gossiped. A bald eagle stood sentinel on the dead top branch of a Douglas fir: "Weep, weep, weep," he called, and then wheeled through the forest to another perch, white tail flashing. In the evening, stuffed with salmon, we watched the sun go down behind Nootka Island. A great wedge of sea fog stole up Zuciarte Channel, highlighting the mountains of Bligh Island and blotting out those of the mainland behind.

Next morning was overcast, but there was no wind as we paddled along to Tahsis Inlet and up to the old Mowachaht winter village of Coopte. Completely overgrown, we found it hard to believe that, in 1792, it was the site of the colourful potlatch ceremony Moziño describes in *Noticias de Nutka*. Apparently, somebody still goes there, as decayed lawn chairs had been thrown in the bush and a bag of trail food lay abandoned behind a log. An offering to the squirrels, perhaps? Returning to Hoiss, we packed quickly. We tried again to make it into the hidden lake, but, once more, we were foiled by the tide and proceeded to Hisnet Inlet.

At the head of the inlet, the tide had flooded the flat area where we thought we could camp. Reluctant to go further, we squeezed our tents in between the shafts of the old limestone quarry, which, nearly a century ago, supplied stone for the Parliament buildings in Victoria. It was one of those unlucky nights when the rain bucketed down. We tried to ignore it and had fun combining several large tarps into a shelter at one end of the fire. The wind started to gust, and the third time it doused the flames we retreated to warm sleeping bags. All night

**Why do Tugs and Barges Take Lumber in Both Directions?**

*It's not the same lumber. Each mill specialises in processing certain types of wood and any species which it can't process is shipped off to the Vancouver Log Exchange. There the wood is exchanged for a kind which the mill* **can** *process. No money changes hands, though the transactions are based on market value. The actual exchange takes place in Howe Sound, an inlet near Vancouver (Tahsis sends yellow cedar, which is exchanged for red cedar).*

the wind blew like an express train. A few unfortunates were heard groping their way in the darkness, teetering on the quarry's edge while restaking tent pegs. Others listened snug in their warm bags.

Next morning, I thought the little dog, Curly, seemed uneasy, but, new to bush camping, I hesitated to voice my fears. Why risk having these experienced campers laugh at my concerns? Three of us paddled over to Deserted River for a short hike up to the lake where a pair of loons called a welcome. On the way back, my friend, Dorothy, claimed Wendy had talked in her sleep during the night. The grunts and growls Dorothy described didn't sound like a person, but again I said nothing. Suddenly, we heard the others shouting and yodelled in reply. We paddled back to camp to find the rest waiting for us in their canoes about six metres off shore.

"A cougar came and took Curly," they explained. "Bob was standing within three metres of the fire with Curly close by when he heard a sound and saw the cat with Curly in its mouth. He rushed after it, hollering and thrashing around in the bush, losing his watch in the process. Don joined him and the cougar must have thought there was too much competition because it dropped Curly and took off. Your gear is all on shore." Curly had a couple of small teeth-marks on his shoulder but was otherwise unharmed, although understandably subdued. Although cougars definitely live here, most people who visit Hisnet Inlet will never see one. It's a good idea to leave dogs at home and to keep a close watch on small children.

## III. Little Espinosa Inlet to Catala Island

Four of us — Bud, Ray, Lorne, and myself, all in sea kayaks — put in by the bridge separating the two halves of Little Espinosa Inlet. Being new to the West Coast, we got up late and launched about 11:00 a.m. After a beautiful paddle down the narrow inlet, we lunched on a grassy meadow, where Little Espinosa joins its big namesake.

After lunch, each paddled at his or her own pace, and we occasionally met at designated points. Bud zigzagged across the inlet; Lorne, the newest paddler, went from point to point; and Ray and I followed the shore to admire great globs of purple starfish, brown and white anemones, and the occasional scarlet blood starfish. By the time we reached the entrance to Esperanza Inlet, a wind had got up making it impossible to cross to Garden Point.

Not knowing we could sneak up the side of Esperanza to camp at Graveyard Bay, we crossed Espinosa and camped at Newton Cove, which has no comfortable place to pitch a tent. Bud was wise and, after first pitching his tent in a streambed, moved it to a rocky outcrop above the vegetation and promptly fell fast asleep, missing all the later excitement. Though at least two of the rest of us should have known better, we ignored the warning of the sea asparagus plant, which grows on the high-tide line, and made camp on top of it at the edge of the shingle.

Exhausted, I went to sleep about 9:30 p.m. Shortly afterwards, I heard Lorne's voice outside: "You better get up, the tide's within three inches of your tent and it's got another two hours to come up." Hastily, we repitched the two tents on the rocky shore just below the sleeping Bud. At 11:00 p.m., Lorne's voice was heard again: "I'm floating and you probably are too." I was.

Stumbling around in the dark, we repitched Ray's tent in the only place we could — on top of the stream bed where Bud's tent had been. In the morning, my abandoned tent had thirty centimetres of water in it. We've never ignored sea asparagus since.

Our next campsite had everything that Newton Cove did not. Garden Point on the south side of Esperanza Inlet, is a B.C. Forest campsite, and it has a pit toilet, space to pitch about five tents under some truly massive cedar trees, and a wonderful spit of shell beach, which stretches out to a tiny island garnished with shore pines. Other offshore islands shelter the beach from the wind, so we spread out our wet tents, sleeping bags, and clothes. Twenty minutes later the hot sun had dried it all. In the afternoon, as the water shimmered from green to blue, we swam in the warm shallows. A supper stew of our combined resources (orchestrated by Bud and topped off with

*Kayaker coming through a sea cave on Catala Island.*

Ray's special chocolate pudding), together with a good night's sleep, banished memories of our previous troubles.

Rising at dawn, we again paddled along the shore. The uninhabited First Nations Reserve at the mouth of Owossitsa Creek hides a mossy rainforest wonderland a few metres further up. A tiny white-shell sand beach below a patch of short green grass marks the entrance. There is reputed to be a trail to Owossitsa Lake here, but we didn't find it. Now that the Flynn property has been logged, the easiest way to get to Owossitsa Lake is to go one kilometre up the logging road.

Trashed and decayed, the Flynn cabin still stood. Exploring it, we found a grouse that appeared tame. A descendent of the Minniebelle Bethine Flynn describes in her book? We like to think so.

At the mouth of the inlet, we crossed to Catala Island. After three hours of paddling from Garden Point, we were glad to reach a gravel beach on the north side and to set up camp. The big flat meadow has lots of tent space. Water from several streams on the mainland opposite can be boiled if you run out of your own supply. We spent a week here fishing and exploring the offshore beaches and islets.

At low tide, we snorkelled in search of rare purple scallops and gathered shellfish and seaweed for evening meals. When a commercial fish boat anchored by the camp, we negotiated a salmon which we cooked in foil and served with garlic-fried sea asparagus. Dessert was a slice of my imported no-bake cheese cake.

One solo side trip around Tatchu Point gave me more than I bargained for. After a night camped at Yellow Bluff, a beautiful sandy crescent beach, I started for the point in the dark calm before sunrise, wearing my wetsuit and with all safety equipment reachable from the cockpit. Within thirty minutes, wind and waves forced me back to a day of beachcombing and waterfall showers at Peculiar Point. In the evening calm, I made it back to Catala. Bud, who had rounded Tatchu once before and who required three days rest to recover from it, said: "I told you so!"

On the return journey, we slipped into Queen Cove at the entrance to Port Eliza. A large power boat decorated with radar balls was anchored in the lagoon behind the village. We paddled down to inspect it and met Harold Amis from the reserve in a handsome Nuu-chah-nulth canoe which he had built himself. Black outside and scarlet inside, it had the traditional wolf ears on the bow. These canoes were so well built that, before the Europeans came, they were exported to tribes on the east coast of Vancouver Island. As we paddled back, Harold showed us where to camp on the east side of Queen Cove and invited us to cook supper at his house. Since then, when frying potatoes I always mix in chopped onion and lots of black pepper and salt — Harold style. Next morning, the *Uchuck* met us at Frank Beban's dock and let us debark again at the mouth of Zeballos Inlet. A couple of hours later, we were reunited with the vehicles we had left at the Zeballos dock.

## IV. The Head of Muchalat Inlet

The head of Muchalat Inlet gets few visitors because most of the traffic travels down the Inlet to Nootka Sound. On a still day at the end of October, I skimmed through a mysterious land clothed in uninterrupted dark forest — cedar, fir, hemlock, and spruce. Above me, the 1,220-metre peaks of the Pierce Range reared their heads. They commemorate Lieutenant Thomas Pierce — sometimes spelt Pearce — a British naval officer who hoisted the British flag at Friendly Cove the day the Spaniards left in 1795. Ahead of me, spring salmon tinged with dusky scarlet leapt out of the water in anticipation of spawning.

I skirted the vertical cliffs before rounding a big bend to find a large alluvial fan of gravel from the Burman River. Mount Splendour dominated the scene. From its southern slopes, just over the ridge, the Megin River runs into Clayoquot Sound. Tofino seemed a world away, though, it was only forty-eight kilometres south as the crow flies.

In the Burman River, the wondrous ritual of spawning season attracted a congregation of bald eagles to lofty perches. This was once the location of one of the main villages of the Muchalaht people. Nothing visible remains.

### V. Fair Harbour to Spring Island

With a 6:00 a.m. start, the half-hour paddle to the mouth of sheltered Fair Harbour was calm (as usual), and, though I wanted to linger and explore the nearby islands, I knew that with several crossings to make and few landing places I must move fast. The object: Spring Island, with its lovely wild beaches and trail. Although Kyuquot Sound doesn't have quite as much history as do Nootka Sound and Esperanza Inlet, it does have less traffic and more secluded wilderness. Those who explore it should either be accompanied by a competent guide or be well practised in the arts of wilderness survival and no-impact camping.

Once around the Markale Peninsula, which guards the entrance to Fair Harbour, I crossed over to Hohoae Island and sneaked along the sheltered north shore before crossing to Union Island. There I stopped at the cove behind tiny Chutsis Island for a snack and to admire the old-growth forest. Huge cedar trees shaded large clumps of sword ferns on the forest floor, and blankets of pale green Spanish moss hung from branches. Amongst the grey shingle at the water's edge I noticed the irridescent gleam of an abalone shell.

Paddling into the narrow neck of water between Surprise Island and Union Island, I pictured Captain William Spring anchoring his twenty-eight-ton sealing schooner, the *Surprise*, in this sheltered lagoon in the 1860s while he persuaded Kyuquot men to bring their canoes aboard to hunt seals with him in the Bering Sea.

Across from Surprise Island, I followed the north coast of Crowther Channel into Kyuquot, marvelling at the logistics of living in such a remote village spread over several islands. A fishboat captain filling up with ice at the Co-op in Walters Cove told me to look out for the tame harbour seal, Miss Charlie. Sure enough, she swam in front of me as I approached the government dock. My timing was good, as the store opened almost immediately and everyone seemed to be there to get their mail.

Opposite Walters Cove and the government dock is the Houpsitas Reserve, where most of the Kyuquot people now live. East of it is well-concealed McKay Cove (named after Captain Hugh McKay, a partner of Captain Spring). The cove has two hazards — a shallow, rock-studded entrance (which prevents many boats from accessing it) and 1.25 metre overfalls (which are created during very low tides, when the entrance drains). There were no overfalls that day, just a rather dull-looking big lake, so I retreated to take pictures of the pretty Red Cross Field Hospital where a friend of mine had worked.

Leaving Kyuquot behind, I crossed Nicholaye Channel to the Mission Group. As I drifted past Aktis Island, I pictured the excitement on the dark night in 1855 when a group of southern tribes attacked, and were repelled by, the brave Kyuquot. Behind Aktis is Spring Island, where I camped and met Rupert Wong, who, from May to September, operates West Coast Expeditions. He has a permanent camp of tents on wooden pads and a large tarpaulin-covered kitchen facility. Wong, a marine biologist, believes in immersing his guests in the wonders of the natural world, and he schedules sessions with Kyuquot elders so that one may hear their stories. Consequently, his program is very popular, especially with seniors.

Respect for native lands and issues is very important to Wong. As he says: "People should not land on Indian Reserves without permission. Recognise that, to the Kyuquot peoples, they own all the land from Rugged Point to the Brooks Peninsula and back into the inlets to the height of land. To get permission, write to the Kyuquot Band and then only for day use at village sites. Mortuary sites are tabu. B.C. Parks will be coming out with some signage which will be seen at Fair Harbour and on the *Uchuck*."

In the morning, I watched Wong's student kayakers learn to paddle while I ate breakfast. Overhead, a hungry osprey chick cheeped continually. After browsing through Wong's reference library, consisting largely of natural history books, I spent the day renewing my acquaintance with the beaches on the far side of the island (where a friend and I were once stormbound for a day).

We gathered up all the plastic trash on the beach and burnt it. Then we scrambled around the adjacent beaches looking for green glass balls. Someone must have been there before us because all we found was one piece of glass with some Japanese characters on it. I looked again this time but found nothing. To be successful, you have to be first on the beach after a big storm; you also have to be lucky, as more plastic floats than glass floats are now used.

Early next morning, out in the middle of Nicholaye Channel in a soft, pearl-grey world of sea and sky, I heard faint clicks. A sea otter was using a pebble to break open a sea urchin. These otters are very shy and hard to approach. Camera buffs will need at least a 300-millimetre lense to get anything more than a dot in the middle of their picture. In 1969, a small colony of these almost-extinct animals was transplanted from Alaska to the Bunsby Islands, six nautical miles north of Kyuquot. Many kayakers make the pilgrimage to see them. The colony flourished, and now the otters have spread along the coast and are frequently seen eating sea urchins in the kelp beds between Amos Island and the Mission Group.

South of Union Island, I looked longingly towards the tiny Thornton Islands decorated with wispy shore pines. I have heard that they give all who visit the impression that they are the first people to have done so. Those who climb to the top find themselves looking down into an eagle's nest. Unfortunately, the weather forecast was poor, so I headed for Rugged Point.

Rugged Point, at the entrance to Kyuquot Channel, is a very popular camping place for small boaters and a good anchorage for yachts (except in a north wind). Both the inner and outer beaches are sandy. A trail connecting them winds through the forest and past a quaint, pack-rat-infested log cabin, which has beside it, of all things, a sauna.

As I hiked along the outer beaches looking for bits of dentalia shells, I thought of the Kyuquot and the Ehattesaht people who inherited the rights to harvest them from the deep waters off shore. Locations and methods were closely guarded family secrets and were ritualistically passed on from one generation to the next. Secrecy was essential as strings of dentalia shells were used as money, thus owning harvesting rights was akin to owning your own gold mine.

After a night at Rugged Point, I paddled up Kyuquot Channel, stopping to relax in the sunshine below a cormorant nesting site on a high cliff on the south side of Hohoae Island. From there I looked into the mouth of Cachalot Inlet, where a whaling station had operated from 1908 to 1926. It employed eighty men and exported oil to Ohio to aid in the manufacture of soap.

Kyuquot Sound has been the scene of several attempts to mine gold and copper. In the 1940s, Amai Inlet, then known as Deep Inlet, had three shafts up to 457-metres above sea level; these were used in the excavation of gold and the company which used them brought in a gondola to facilitate the process. In addition, claims were staked for gold on the Artlish River, but the ore wasn't of a high enough grade to make it worth mining. The head of Kashutl Inlet, near the 1.6-kilometre-long Caledonia Falls, contains the remains of some buildings which, in the early 1900s, were part of a copper claim.

Perhaps the rusted remains of an old anchor which I found at the north end of Hohoae Island were a legacy of some of this activity. I hurriedly left, as the wind was freshening and I wanted to get across Pinnace Channel. On the other side, I considered portaging into Fair Harbour over the narrow neck of land where once the Kyuquot winter village of Markale stood, but I opted to paddle around instead.

After I had unloaded my boat at Fair Harbour, I lingered, watching some Kyuquot residents using the crane on the dock to load a heavy engine. At that moment, any excuse would do; I felt so reluctant to leave for another year.

## VII. Circumnavigation of Nootka Island

Since my arthritis prevents me from making surf landings, I have never made this trip, but know people who have. Take the *Uchuck* to Friendly Cove, camp the night there, rise early, and paddle up Tahsis Inlet to camp the second night at Esperanza.

Individuals and small groups are welcome to camp at Esperanza and, in exchange for a donation, have meals at the dining hall. A special campsite for kayakers and canoeists has been cleared in the woods just east of the main dock, and a trail connects it to the settlement. Since you'll arrive tired, consider spending two nights here to explore the mission, Ceepeecee, McBride Bay (where there are the remains of a cannery), and God's Pocket in Hecate Channel.

Haven Cove, which is affectionately called God's Pocket by the locals, is on the west side of Hecate Channel near Steamer Point. I have fond memories of my last visit there. The pines on the small islets at its entrance caught the sun as I approached by kayak. Inside the cove, all was still and green, and a friendly seal quietly came up to inspect me. On a sunny day, when, elsewhere the afternoon winds are raging, the still green waters of this pretty cove enable one to

*Third Beach on Nootka Island is usually pounded by Pacific Ocean swells.*

understand how it got its name. The northwest corner contains a one-tent campsite and a brick fire circle beside a stream. Up the hill behind, the trunks of the cedar trees bear scars left when Ehattesaht women stripped them of some of their bark.

Mothers and grandmothers taught young girls how to select a suitable tree. The grain of the bark had to run straight up the trunk without twisting. They would say a prayer and then, about one metre from the ground, make a horizontal cut and a third of the way around the tree. Slowly and carefully, using a wedge, they pulled a long strip of bark (up to nine metres) away from the trunk. After drying, the bark was beaten and separated into layers. Many of the trees used for this purpose can still be identified by the long scar up their trunks, (they usually face up a slope, as this made it easier to pull off the bark). Archaeologists refer to them as CMTs — culturally modified trees. The Western red cedar was the most popular with the Nuu-chah-nulth who used every part of it to build houses and canoes, to catch fish, and to make clothing, baskets, and storage boxes.

Leaving Esperanza, head for the Garden Point campsite but stop en route at Ehatisaht on the north side of the inlet. This was once the main village of the people who dominated Esperanza Inlet. Their descendants now live outside Zeballos. Only graves remain at the village site. Because of the shortage of campsites in the area, tourists sometimes camp at the cemetery, but Ehattesaht band members (who frequently travel the inlet) will ask campers to leave. You can camp at the east end of Graveyard Bay, less than a mile west of Ehatisaht. It used to contain a wooden cross in memory of Bill Smith, an Ehattesaht band member, but this is no longer visible.

If you reach Garden Point too early to stop, and the weather is good, proceed on to the islands on the south side of Nuchatlitz and make camp on the first one you come to. It may be windy, but it puts you in a good position to cross Nuchatlitz Inlet as early as possible. Avoid the combination of an ebb tide and a westerly wind *(see Hazards Chapter 6)*. As you head for Ferrer Point, watch for herds of sea otters around the skerries.

The first sandy beach past Ferrer Point is Third Beach. There is less surf if you land at the north end. Calvin Creek and Beano Creek are also popular sandy beaches upon which to land, but they require surf skills. A lucky Scottish kayaker, on his first trip to Canada, saw a wolf cub at Calvin Creek. It disappeared but came out again when he whistled. As he snapped a picture, all its kin replied with a chorus of howls. Another group saw a very large black bear on this beach, so they didn't camp there (though many do).

Fast paddlers can probably make it from Nuchatlitz all the way to Friendly Cove in a day, but this is like doing Europe in a week. Stop a while and enjoy the sun — and make sure you have several extra days' food with you in case you get stormbound.

If you're capable of this trip and can do an eddy turn, you may enjoy some of the white-water described trips in Chapter 5.

## THE LEGACY — SOMETHING TO THINK ABOUT

When you've explored Nootka Sound and its surrounding waterways by boat, you understand why the First Nations people used the water as their main transportation route. However, while our boats are merely trusted vessels of transport, their canoes are that and more. Built from 400 to 800-year-old cedar trees, the First Nations peoples believe their canoes embody the spirits of the trees from which they are made. Since 1985, First Nations peoples along the coast have revived the art of building ocean-going canoes (up to fifteen metres in length) as they regenerate their culture.

Today's world is as tied up with lawyer's jargon and bureaucratic red tape as was that of the eighteenth century Spaniards who settled Nootka. Perhaps we all need to embody the spirit of the canoe. The First Nations peoples can help us regenerate more than their own culture.

# APPENDICES

## ACCOMMODATIONS

In addition to the annual *British Columbia Accommodations* obtain listings of B&Bs, fishing charters, and so on from the tourist infocentre at Gold River and the village offices at Tahsis and Zeballos. **Note: Effective in October, 1996, the Telephone Area Code in this region switches from 604 to 205.**

### R.V. SITES:

#### Gold River

***Peppercorn Trail Motel and R.V. Site*** at Gold River. Close to a hundred sites are either on the river or have beautiful views of the Matchlee Glacier. Electrical, sewage, water, and Cable TV hookups, showers and a laundromat on site. Close to the municipal aquatic centre (with three pools and a sauna) and the nine-hole golf course. Since the site is fully occupied most of the year by construction workers, it is recommended that you make reservations two to four weeks in advance.

***Gold River Lions Campsite*** South of the Village of Gold River, between the rushing water of the Gold River and Highway 28. No hook-ups. Water and pit toilets. First come first served, often full by 3 p.m.

#### Tahsis

***Tahsis Peppermill R.V. Site*** near Captain Meares School has power, sewer, and Cable TV hook-ups for twenty sites. Beside the river, excellent view of Rugged Mountain. Reservations recommended.

*Moutcha Bay,* a private operation on the road to Tahsis, it is being developed slowly. With its own boat launch on Tlupana Inlet, this is a less crowded alternative to Cougar Creek. Bait, snacks, marine gas.

#### Zeballos

**The R.V. site on Parkway Road** has four pads, with water, sewer, and power hook-ups. There is a sani-dump, public washroom, and laundry facilities. Sites are available on a first-come first-served basis (a small charge is levied by the village of Zeballos). Though not on the river or the inlet, you do get mountain views all round.

**The Cevallos campsite on the Zeballos River** has water but no hook-ups. Stays are limited to two weeks, and there is no reservation system.

**Other popular sites, though there are no hook-ups, include:**

- B.C. Forest campsites at Cougar Creek, Leiner River, Muchalat Lake, Vernon Lake.
- Others at Conuma River and Fair Harbour.

## CAMPSITES

### Accessible by Road

Many people car-camp and tent at the R.V. sites listed above. In addition, West Bay at Tahsis has six tent sites.

### Accessible by Water Only

**Garden Point** on Esperanza Inlet is a B.C. Forest campsite with a pit toilet and a river for fresh water (if you hike up beyond the saltiness of the high tide).

**Esperanza Mission** In exchange for a donation, you can get permission to camp in designated areas, use the showers, and eat at the communal dining lounge. The store at the dock has chocolate bars and pop.

**Friendly Cove** The Mowachaht Band has designated a camping area near the cabins. Pit toilets. Take your own water.

**Wilderness campsites suitable for more than three tents:** Catala Island and Hoiss (Be sure to hang food well out of reach of the black bears which sometimes come to Hoiss. Never feed the bears).

## USEFUL CONTACTS:

**AIR NOOTKA, LTD.,**

Box 19, Gold River, B.C. V0P 1G0. (Open 7 days/week).
Phone (604) 283–2255 Fax (604) 283–2256.
Scheduled trips to Tahsis & Kyuquot 3 days a week.
Cessna 180 and Beaver available for sightseeing trips at hourly rates.

**CAMPBELL RIVER FISH AND WILDLIFE ASSOCIATION**

For information on archery hunting.
Box 271, Campbell River, B.C. V9W 5B1

**EHATTESAHT BAND**

P.O. Box 716, 938 Island Highway, Campbell River, B.C. V9W 6J3.
Phone (604) 287–4353.

**GOLD RIVER TRAVEL INFOCENTRE**

1 Highway 28, Gold River, B.C. V0P 1G0.
Phone (604) 283–2418.

**KYUQUOT BAND**

General Delivery, Kyuquot, B.C. V0P 1J0.
Phone (604) 332–5259

**MOWACHAHT BAND**

Box 459, Gold River, B.C. V0P 1G0.
Phone (604) 283–2532 or (604)283–7522, Fax (604)283–2335.

**NOOTKA SOUND SERVICE LTD, (M.V. UCHUCK)**

P.O. Box 57, Gold River, B.C. V0P 1G0.
Phone: Office (604) 283–2515, Ship (604)283–2325, Fax (604)283–7582.

***Air Nootka Flights***

*Five days a week, Air Nootka float planes leave Gold River for Tahsis and Kyuquot, taking the mail, passengers, and other freight. For those who can afford it, the round-trip flight takes 3.25 hours and is a quick way to get an overview of the many inlets and waterways. The flights to Tahsis and Kyuquot follow the inlets, as does the Uchuck; and like the ship, the float planes may take unscheduled side-trips to remote logging operations. On a clear day, both the approach and departure from Tahsis provide you with a good view of Rugged Mountain (1,876 metres), which has snow on it most of the year. Between early February and mid-April, at the mouth of Esperanza Inlet, watch for whales migrating northwards. As you approach Kyuquot, you see the Brooks Peninsula and the northern part of Vancouver Island in the distance. Close under you is the Mission Group of islands and Kyuquot itself. At Kyuquot you land at Air Nootka's dock a few metres away from the government dock and the general store. The return trip may follow the same route but sometimes returns direct to Gold River passing over Nootka Island. Much depends on the freight and on what the passengers want to see.*

*Seventy-five per cent of Air Nootka's work is concerned with charter business. In addition to logging company work, they often go to Vancouver and Seattle to pick up fishing-lodge guests who want to increase their fishing time by several days. Air Nootka has three planes. The Beaver and the twin-engine Dornier take six passengers each, and the Cessna 180 takes three.*

**TAHSIS VILLAGE OFFICE**

977 South Maquinna Drive, P.O. Box 519, Tahsis, B.C. V0P 1X0.
Phone (604) 934–6344, Fax (604) 934–6622

**VANCOUVER ISLAND HELICOPTERS LTD.**

Gold River, B.C. V0P 1G0.
Phone (604) 283–7616

**ZEBALLOS VILLAGE OFFICE**

Box 127, Zeballos, B.C. V0P 2A0.
Phone (604) 761–4229.

## FACILITIES

### CEEPEECEE

B&B, limited boat repairs — call Sousen or Ceepeecee on VHF Channel 6 or phone (604) 934–6674.

### ESPERANZA

Gas, diesel, small store. (No facilities at Fair Harbour.)

### FRIENDLY COVE

Visitor cabins available for rent. Book well in advance at the Mowachaht Band Office in Gold River. Bring food and sleeping bags. Boats may tie up to the Williams' dock for a nominal fee.

### GOLD RIVER

Shopping centre, health clinic, freight and passenger service, sea planes and helicopters, boat and fishing charters, par 71 golf course.

### KYUQUOT

Store with post office and liquor store, gas, diesel, limited B&B facilities in Walters Cove and on Houpsitas Reserve, Red Cross outpost hospital.

### MUCHALAT INLET

Government dock with limited moorage by Avenor Pulp Mill; Petro Canada gas; Air Nootka Office, phone (604) 283–2255. For a cab to Gold River for groceries and other supplies phone (604) 283–2117.

### TAHSIS

Store with post office and liquor store; hotels, motels, and B&Bs; R.V. site; hospital; gas and diesel.

### TLUPANA INLET

**Moutcha Bay Resort** is the only one accessible by road. Has marine gas and small store. Parking is for guests only. Moorage at marina.

**Critter Cove:** Gas, moorage, small restaurant.

**Other fish camps:** For details contact Gold River Travel Infocentre.

### WOSS

Combined gas pump and store. Also, Canfor's Englewood Logging Division. Call 281–2300 before using the Artlish, an active logging road to Kyuquot Sound which is only recommended for car toppers. It cuts about thirty kilometres off the distance but is not well signed. Kyuquot residents use it regularly, but they are used to its twists and turns. They also know that they must drive "by line of sight": this means driving at thirty to forty kilometres per hour so that they have time to stop and pull over when they see a logging truck approaching.

### ZEBALLOS

Gas pump, general store, a bakery, and one or two other stores, plus accommodation and campsite. Meals at the hotel and the bakery. Marine gas, diesel.

## POPULAR SALT-WATER FISHING LOCATIONS

**ESPERANZA INLET**

Catala Island, Rosa Island, Steamer Point, Tahsis Narrows.

**KYUQUOT SOUND**

Fair Harbour, Lookout Island.

**NOOTKA SOUND**

Camel Rock, off Descubierta Point; Hoiss Point; Atrevida Point; San Miguel Islands.

**TAHSIS INLET**

Mouth of the Inlet by Strange Island, Tahsis Narrows (where the tidal flow is constricted).

**TLUPANA INLET**

Coho Point on the east side between Nesook Bay and Cougar Creek, Argonaut Point.

## POPULAR FRESH-WATER FISHING LOCATIONS

**GOLD AND HEBER RIVERS.**

**TAHSIS RIVER, LEINER RIVER, SUCWOA RIVER, CONUMA RIVER, MALASPINA LAKE, PERRY LAKE.**

**MUCHALAT LAKE, VERNON LAKE, NIMPKISH RIVER.**

**ZEBALLOS RIVER, NOMASH RIVER.**

## WHEN TO EXPECT THE FISH

Late April to May, halibut; late July to August, chinook; September to Mid November, coho; December to mid July, immature chinook.
December, March to May, September, steelhead.

## MAPS AND CHARTS

Pacific Forest Products Recreation and Logging Road Guide to the Forest Lands of West Vancouver Island Scale 1:125,000
1 centimetre = 1.25 kilometres (1 inch = 2 miles).

**TOPOGRAPHIC MAPS**

Scale 1: 50,000
Sheets 92 E/15 Zeballos
92 E/16 Gold River
92 L/2 Woss Lake
92 E/9 Muchalat Inlet
92 L/3 Kyuquot
92E/14, for Tatchu Point area

**CHARTS**

3651 Scoular Entrance and Kyuquot — Details entrance to Walters Cove.
3662 Nootka Sound to Esperanza Inlet
3663 Esperanza Inlet
3664 Nootka Sound
3665 Plans — Nootka Sound
3682 Kyuquot Sound

## *Metric Conversions*

Multiply by

|  |  |
|---|---|
| Acres to hectares | 0.4 |
| Hectares to acres | 2.5 |
| Fathoms to metres | 1.8 |
| Metres to fathoms | 0.6 |
| Feet to metres | 0.3 |
| Metres to feet | 3.3 |
| Gallons to Litres | 4.6 |
| Litres to Gallons | 0.2 |
| Inches to centimetres | 2.5 |
| Centimetres to inches | 0.4 |
| Miles to Kilometres | 1.6 |
| Kilometres to Miles | 0.6 |
| Nautical miles to Kilometres | 1.9 |
| Kilometres to Nautical | 0.5 |
| Pounds to Kilograms | 0.5 |
| Kilograms to Pounds | 2.2 |

Fahrenheit to centigrade — subtract 32, multiply by $5/9$

Centigrade to Fahrenheit — multiply by $9/5$, add 32

## FURTHER READING

*B.C. Fishing Adventures; Vancouver Island/Lower Mainland.* Vancouver: Infomap, 199– (annual). ISBN 0-9693607-7-0. Excellent fresh-water fishing reference.

Clark, Cecil. *B.C. Provincial Police Stories.vol.3.* Surrey: Heritage House, 1993. ISBN 0-919214-80-0 (v.3) Includes "Diary of Despair," which chronicles the sad fate of the two trappers who starved to death at Vernon Lake in 1940.

Douglass, Don. *Exploring Vancouver Island's West Coast.* Bishop,Ca: Fine Edge Productions, 1994. ISBN 0-938665-26-X Excellent sketch maps of anchorages. Although Douglass may have seen kayaks ashore where he has marked them at Yellow Bluff, most paddlers will prefer to land at the west end of the crescent beach instead.

*Flynn's Cove.* Sidney: Porthole Press, 1986. ISBN 0-919931-19-3. A veterinarian's widow describes life at Newton Cove on Esperanza Inlet, visits to Nuchatlitz and working at the Christie Indian Residential School.

Guppy, Walter. *Wilderness Wandering on Vancouver Island.* [Place of publication]: Grassroots, 1993. ISBN 0-9697703-0-8 Written by a geologist, it includes a chapter on the Zeballos claims as seen in the 1980s.

Jewitt, John R. *White Slaves of the Nootka; Narrative of the Adventures and Sufferings of John R. Jewitt while a captive on Vancouver Island — 1802–03.* Surrey: Heritage House, 1987. ISBN 0-919214-51-7.

Johnson, Louise. *Not Without Hope: The story of Dr. H. A. McLean and the Esperanza General Hospital.Matsqui:* Maple Lane, 1992. ISBN 0-921066-02-4.

Jones, Laurie. *Nootka Sound Explored; a West Coast History*: Campbell River Ptarmigan Press, 1991. ISBN 0-919537-24-3. A regional history of Nootka and Kyuquot Sounds sponsored by the West Coast Committee of Comox-Strathcona and a companion book to the video of the same name.

Moziño, Jose Mariano Noticias de Nutka; *An account of Nootka Sound in 1792.* Seattle and Vancouver: Univ. Wash. and Douglas & McIntyre, 1970. ISBN 0-295-97103-7. Written by a Spanish botanist-naturalist and translated and edited by Iris H. Wilson Engstrand.

*Pacific Northwest Waggoner.* Bellevue,WA: Weatherly Press, 1996- (annual). ISBN 0-935727-12-4, ISSN 1076-1578. Detailed verbal instructions on accessing various anchorages but lacks sketch maps. The "Nootka Mission" is Esperanza Mission.

Pratt-Johnson, Betty. *Whitewater Trips for Kayakers, Canoeists and Rafters on Vancouver Island.* Vancouver, Gordon Soules, 1984. ISBN 0-919574-67-X. Detailed information about three trips on the Gold River and two on the Nimpkish River.

Watmough, Don. *West Coast of Vancouver Island, Cape Scott to Sooke including Barkley Sound.* Vol 4, *Pacific Yachting's Cruising Guide to British Columbia.* Vancouver: Pacific Yachting, 1984. ISBN 0-88896-147-2 (v.4).

# INDEX

## HISTORICAL CHRONOLOGY

*A Nootka Sound man and Woman as depicted in James Cook's* ***Third Voyage.***

**2300 BC** Earliest archaeological evidence of human settlement.

**1741** Russians Chirikov and Bering explore Alaska and build settlements. Did not venture as far south as Nootka.

**1774** Juan Pérez passes Nootka Sound in the *Santiago* but fails to land.

**1778** Cook lands at Nootka Sound and claims it for British King George III.

**1786** James Charles Strange arrives in *The Experiment.* He leaves his young surgeon, Dr. John Mackay, to write up " . . . the manners, customs, religion and government of the Nootka."

**1787** Captain Charles William Barkley and his wife, Frances, aboard the *Imperial Eagle* purchase furs at Friendly Cove and pick up Dr. John Mackay. Frances is the first white woman to visit the Pacific Northwest. Barkley Sound, further south, is named after them.

**1788** John Meares launches the *Northwest America,* the first European ship built on the coast at Friendly Cove. He later claims to the British Government that he purchased land from Maquinna, triggering the Nootka Controversy.

**1789** The Spanish settle in at Nootka under Martínez, who seizes the *Iphigenia, Meares Northwest America* and two British ships *Argonaut* and *Princess Royal,* causing an incident of international proportion in Europe.

**1791** Alejandro Malaspina visits Nootka.